IMAGES of America
AROUND EAGLE

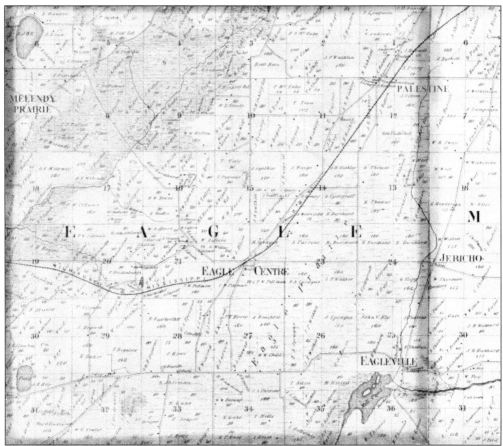

EAGLE 1859 PLAT MAP. This map shows the owners of the land and where they lived represented by the small squares. The town was divided into 36 sections, with each section being a single mile square and consisting of 640 acres. These sections were then further divided into quarter sections of 160 acres and quarter of quarter sections of 40 acres. This map, which will be referenced throughout the book, shows the relationship between the population centers of Eagle Centre, Eagleville, Jericho, Palestine, and Melendy's Prairie. (University of Wisconsin, Milwaukee.)

ON THE COVER. A parade travels down Jericho Street (Main Street) in Eagle Centre (Village of Eagle) in the 1910s. The modern equivalent Kettle Moraine Days began in the 1940s as the Legion Social to raise funds to pay for the American Legion building. It was renamed Kettle Moraine Days in 1962 when the fire department supported it and added a parade. (Sidney Sprague photograph collection.)

IMAGES of America
AROUND EAGLE

Jesse Steinke

Copyright © 2022 by Jesse Steinke
ISBN 978-1-4671-0825-6

Published by Arcadia Publishing
Charleston, South Carolina

Printed in the United States of America

Library of Congress Control Number: 2022934590

For all general information, please contact Arcadia Publishing:
Telephone 843-853-2070
Fax 843-853-0044
E-mail sales@arcadiapublishing.com
For customer service and orders:
Toll-Free 1-888-313-2665

Visit us on the Internet at www.arcadiapublishing.com

SIDNEY SPRAGUE, 1890–1957. In memory of photographer Sidney Sprague. He received his first camera from the Sears and Roebuck catalog in 1906, took a three-week photography class, built a small studio, and photographed Eagle in the early 1900s. Without his collection, this book would not have been possible. He is also the author's great-great-uncle. (Sidney Sprague photograph collection.)

Contents

Acknowledgments		6
Introduction		7
Timeline		10
1.	Prehistoric Eagle	11
2.	Town of Eagle	15
3.	Eagle Centre	31
4.	Lifestyle	45
5.	Farm Life	61
6.	Recreation	77
7.	Civic Life	93
8.	People	109
Bibliography		126
Index		127

ACKNOWLEDGMENTS

I would like to acknowledge Sidney Sprague for taking the photographs, his sister-in-law Mary Sprague née Brady for writing comments on many of them, and his niece June Steinke née Sprague for preserving the photographs and sharing them with her descendants. Thanks go to June's son John Steinke, my father, for sharing the many details and having a love of history and knowledge of Eagle that he shared with me, growing my own passion. Without these people taking and preserving the photographs, I wouldn't have had the material to start the book.

Also of high value were Elaine Ledrowski, the Eagle Historical Society, and the many people who have contributed to the museum over the years. While I had a variety of photographs, their records and additional photographs were able to fill in the gaps in Eagle's story that I didn't have.

In addition, thanks to the many people who have contributed details of photographs and proofed the book to make it as historically accurate as possible. With such a passage of time from when these photographs were taken, it is almost impossible to ensure complete accuracy. A few include Ryan Hajewski, Felicia McWilliams-Froschmayer, Roxanne Raduechel-Butler, and Vivienne Steinke.

I also credit the US Navy for instilling discipline and a sense of duty in me. When I rediscovered the Sprague photo albums, I knew that they needed to be shared with the families of Eagle, and I took on the challenge of documenting as many details as possible before more were lost to time.

Images in this volume appear courtesy of Eagle Historical Society (EHS), Waukesha County Historical Society (WCHS), Wisconsin Department of Natural Resources (WDNR), and other sources as stated. If a source is not identified, the image is from Sidney Sprague's photograph collection in the care of his brother's descendants, the Steinke family.

INTRODUCTION

This book began in my grandmother's attic in 2018. I grew up with an interest in genealogy due to eight generations of my ancestors living in Eagle, going back to 1842. I helped farm the same land that the previous six generations farmed, creating a strong attachment to the town. We sold pumpkins and sweet corn and had a greenhouse where I was never surprised when a second, third, or fourth cousin would stop by to chat. Each time, my dad would explain the relationship but struggled to remember all of the connections. Finally, around 2010, I decided to document all these family ties and gather as much information as I could while my grandparents were still alive. In 2018, I was trying to overcome dead ends when I remembered some photo albums from my childhood that had names written on the pages. I asked my grandmother about them, and she sent me up into the attic to look for them. I only remembered three albums, but to my surprise, I found 13 albums with over 3,000 photographs in them. I was mesmerized by these albums, realizing what a treasure they were. Going through them, I found plenty of family photographs that helped me with my genealogical research, but I was also shocked by how many photos were of various areas and families of Eagle and the surrounding areas. These photographs deserved so much more than being forgotten while sitting in an attic gathering dust, and needed to be shared. I took on the task to scan them and share them with people. While sharing them I started learning more details about the town and the stories behind some of the photographs. Unfortunately, I also discovered that many of the details and stories behind the images had already been lost to time. I realized I was battling with time to document the stories and the details of the photographs, so I decided to publish as many of the images and details that I could find to share with the widest possible audience.

Unfortunately, this book was only able to fit a small portion of the photographs, their details, and the town's history. Hopefully, it is just the beginning.

This book begins much further back than some comparable titles, but Eagle's prehistoric and geological details are important to understand the reasons the pioneers settled here, how that terrain supported their success, and how it makes Eagle such an interesting and unique town.

Around 420 million years ago, portions of the states of Michigan, Illinois, and Wisconsin were covered by an inland sea whose western shoreline ran through what is now Eagle. This inland sea became covered by sediments that hardened over time and turned into dolomite rock (historically called limestone) and became known as the Niagara Escarpment. This escarpment is a 650-mile-long discontinuous bedrock ridge that circles the great lakes traveling through Eagle, Kettle Moraine State Forest, High Cliff State Park, Door County, up and around the Great Lakes, and back down to Niagara Falls. This rock provided building materials for early settlers and is still quarried. It also filtered and held clean water, which provided pioneers springs for drinking water and wells for subsequent settlers. To this day, lucky homeowners tap into this aquifer to obtain its great-tasting crystal clear water. I was fortunate to grow up with this water, but my grandparents' house, only 1,000 feet away, did not and tapped instead into terrible-tasting, high-iron water.

Between 75,000 and 10,000 years ago, a series of mile-high glaciers covered most of Wisconsin, eroding much of the softer soils and exposing the Niagara Escarpment. They also scoured the bedrock, breaking it into smaller rocks, gravel, sand, and soil. The glaciers produced lakes, marshes, prairies, kettles (depressions), moraines (accumulations of glacial till), drumlins (hills), and eskers (ridges) that still shape the landscape of Eagle. Without the glaciers, Eagle would look like southwestern Wisconsin's driftless region and would not have been suitable for farming.

After the glaciers receded, various Native American tribes arrived. Very little is known of the earliest people, but arrowheads from 10,000 years ago have been found on the Clarence Armstrong farm in Eagle. The earliest recordings mention the Winnebago (Ho-Chunk) living in the area until the Potawatomi tribes arrived in the early 1700s. The tribes tended to be nomadic and followed the food throughout the area but would settle for the summers and plant corn, beans, and squash. A Native American summer village was in Mukwonago, but evidence suggests Eagle was primarily a hunting ground from the large number of artifacts and arrowheads found through the years. The Native Americans lived in the area until 1833, when they ceded their lands after the Black Hawk War. Wandering bands would return every spring for the next 25 years. After the Black Hawk War, the Wisconsin territory was opened for settlement, and pioneers and speculators began to trickle in.

When Wisconsin became a territory in the spring of 1836, speculators, pioneers, and settlers began to pour into the state trying to be the first to get to the new, inexpensive land. They typically came through the chain of Great Lakes connecting the eastern seaboard to Milwaukee and Green Bay. At that time, Milwaukee was little more than a marsh, with Soloman Junea's trading post. Milwaukee was the county seat of Milwaukee County, which stretched from lake Michigan to Madison and the state line to West Bend. Any land claims made in the 1830s had to be taken to Milwaukee, a 40-mile trip from Eagle through harsh terrain with no roads. Many claims were won only because someone made it to Milwaukee first.

Pioneers settled into the areas around the small hamlets of Palestine, Jericho, Eagleville, and Melendy's Prairie. These hamlets were mostly self-sufficient, with stores, salons, schools, blacksmiths, churches, creameries, and mills. Once the railroad was built, the hamlets were stifled, and Eagle Centre became the town's center. (This book uses the British spelling "Centre" as it is labeled on historical maps.) It was much easier and cheaper to bring in necessary supplies by the railroad than through muddy, rutted, and snow-covered roads.

In 1870, Waukesha County had a population of 28,258, with 35 percent of the population being foreign-born. Of the foreigners, 44 percent were from Germany, 21 percent from England and Wales, 16 percent from Ireland, and small percentages from Scotland, Sweden, Denmark, France, and Holland.

The first settlers in Eagle were primarily the Methodist English. Following them were the Catholics, first the Germans and then the Irish. A story has been passed down that seems more of a generalization than an accurate narrative: the Yankees (New Englanders) liked the open prairies where they could have large farms with little preparation, used up the fertile soils and moved to the next place. The Germans were longer-term settlers who liked farmland mixed with forests for building material and heat sources. They aimed to clear one acre of land per year to improve their farms. The Irish came last and moved into the still vacant, poorer lands of the marshes and hills, much of which was repurchased by the state to form the Southern Kettle Moraine.

One exception was the Yankee Dr. Frederick Sprague, whose family is still on the prairie. He wrote to his brother in Massachusetts in 1842:

> My farm is well watered and has about 160 acres that there is not a bush or stump nor stone on, level and smooth and every foot is as rich as the richest garden there is in Massachusetts. It is very healthy here. There has not been a case of fever of any kind on this prairie since I came here, and the inhabitants indeed seem to know nothing about sickness. The prairie on which I live is a complete flower garden every week and almost every day from the first of March to the first of October. There is a new kind of flower

coming forth; sometimes the prairie is a beautiful blue, sometimes pink, sometimes yellow, and sometimes white with flowers almost all of which are new to me. There is plenty of government land to be sold here for one dollar and twenty-five cents per acre, but will all soon be in secured hands.

Eagle continued to grow through the years, in large part due to transportation. Jericho began as a resting place for oxen drivers. The early farmers raised sheep and wheat due to wool being more durable to ship via slow methods and the wheat being used for flour and grain locally. With the introduction of the railroad, farmers could ship more perishable goods like milk to the large city markets. The many springs within Eagle provided inexpensive cool water to chill the milk and water the animals. Small creameries started up near the farms to turn excess milk into cheese and butter, which had a longer shelf life.

The improved transportation allowed the US Postal Service to offer Rural Free Delivery in the late 1800s. No longer did rural people need to go into town each week to get their mail and shop; they could order the things they needed in catalogs such as Sears and Roebuck. This had an effect on the local boot, shoe, hat, clothing, and tin makers, since people could buy less expensive, mass-produced wares.

As automobiles became more prevalent, wagon shops, liveries, and blacksmiths turned into garages to fix the new, unreliable vehicles. Roads began to be covered in gravel in the early 1900s and were paved by the 1950s. The paving of highways increased the distance goods could be shipped as well as transportation speeds. Cheese factories were consolidated, with the milk being shipped farther. Other businesses like the lumber yard, meat market, drug, hardware and grocery stores went out of business since people could drive to supermarkets to do all their shopping in one place. Since people could drive farther, country living was no longer just for farmers, causing urban sprawl and once again speculators buying land for future developments.

The village of Eagle has changed significantly over the years, and it could have its own book outlining all the changes of what businesses each building held over the year. Buildings would be erected and then expanded upon, fires would burn them down, they would be replaced, or new businesses would move into them. An Eagle Centre business directory in 1873 only lists a mill, a hotel, a saloon, a dry goods store, a doctor, and a carriage maker. In 1894, it had four saloons, two mills, two grocery stores, two hardware stores, two blacksmiths, two hotels, two meat markets, two boot/shoemakers, a harness shop, a wagon shop, a livery, a tailor, a paint shop, a beer-bottling plant, a cheesemaker, a millinery (hat maker), and a lumber yard.

Timeline

- 1832 Black Hawk War
- 1836 Palestine, Jericho, and Eagleville settled.
- 1837 Jerry Parsons builds a hotel in Jericho for weary travelers between Milwaukee and the "Western Wilderness."
- 1838 Census lists 70 people and 18 families in Genesee, with about half of them in the future Eagle.
- 1839 Mukwonago becomes its own town, leaving Eagle as part of Genesee.
- 1840 The first school begins in Jericho.
- 1841 Eagle becomes its own town, taking its name from a large bald eagle seen over the prairie lands. 1841 School built in Palestine, District 1.
- 1842 Store and blacksmith shop built in Palestine.
- 1844 Store and post office built in Eagleville.
- 1846 Waukesha becomes its own county, finalizing the land boundaries of Eagle.
- 1848 Wisconsin becomes a state, many people leave for California gold rush.
- 1849 Ward School, District 3 built.
- 1850 Census lists 796 people, Village Schoolhouse in District 9 built.
- 1851 Milwaukee & St. Paul Railroad laid, with a stop creating Eagle Centre.
- 1852 Crimean War causes wheat prices to skyrocket.
- 1853 Eagle Centre's hotel built.
- 1860 Census lists 1,295 people.
- 1861–1865 Civil War
- 1875 Creamery built in Eagle Centre.
- 1876 Diamond found on Diamond Hill, leading to land speculation.
- 1896 Rural Free Delivery begins.
- 1899 Eagle Centre becomes incorporated as the Village of Eagle.
- 1902 Eagle's telephone company begins.
- 1908 Ford Model T enters production, beginning the automobile revolution.
- 1917–1918 US involvement in World War I.
- 1922 Village of Eagle receives electricity.
- 1930s Rural farms receive electricity.
- 1929–1939 Great Depression
- 1941–1945 US involvement in World War II.

One
Prehistoric Eagle

The Town of Eagle has a lot of history, even before the pioneers made their first claims. During the most recent glacial period from 26,000 to 10,000 years ago, the glaciers separated along the Niagara Escarpment, forming two lobes. What is now Eagle was at the southern limit of these two lobes, where the glaciers extended and retracted numerous times to create the town's many unique geographical features. The glaciers removed sediments that were above the dolomite and created large deposits of aggregates, which were both critical for the settlement and population growth of nearby areas. They provided inexpensive building materials and lime for fertilizer and making concrete. The area is still dotted with quarries excavating this stone. These glaciers also transported the 16-carat diamond that was found near where the water tower now sits when a well was dug in 1876.

After the glaciers, a thin layer of topsoil settled over the gravel and created Eagle Prairie. Strong winds and fires would routinely purge the flatlands of vegetation, maintaining a grassland. In the protected areas, forests sprang up and provided shelter for animals and Native Americans, and provided lumber for the earliest pioneers.

The nearby Native Americans were known to be a friendly tribe who frequently furnished early settlers with shelter, food, guides, and warnings of the movements of hostile tribes.

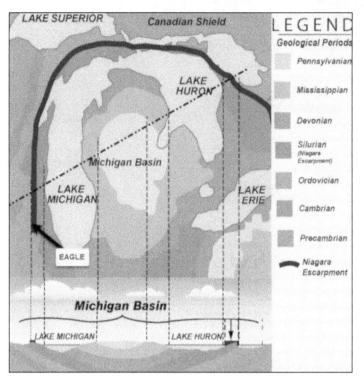

NIAGARA ESCARPMENT. This image outlines the Niagara Escarpment and shows a cross-section of its location under Michigan. The escarpment was critical to the early settlement of Eagle by providing freshwater springs and building materials. The stone was used for roads and buildings, and lime was a critical ingredient in the production of mortar, cement, and fertilizer. (Canadian Geoscience Education Network.)

EAGLE'S GLACIAL PERIOD. The glaciers between 75,000 and 11,000 years ago greatly changed the Eagle area by creating marshes, hills, and prairies. This image shows how the glaciers split because of the Niagara Escarpment, with Waukesha County outlined in the inset. (Wisconsin Geological and Natural History Survey University of Wisconsin-Madison, modified from Luczaj, 2013.)

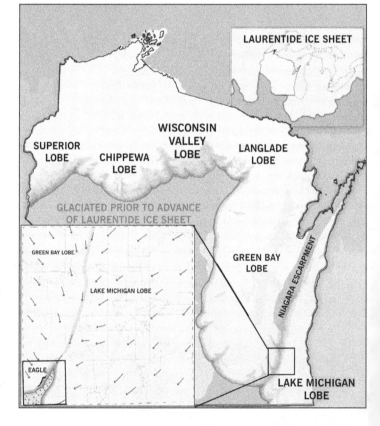

BRADY'S ROCKS. The Niagara Escarpment breaches the surface along the Ice Age Trail about two miles north of the village. The rocky area was named after Irish immigrant Michael Brady (1817–1881, the author's great-great-great-grandfather) who quarried the stone for building material in the town. In the 1960s, the land was purchased by the state as part of the Kettle Moraine Outdoor Recreation Act. (EHS.)

EAGLE DIAMOND. In 1876, a 16.25-carat diamond was found while digging a well near the present water tower. Thinking it was topaz, the family sold it to a jeweler for $1. The stone was sold to Tiffany's for $850 and later to J.P. Morgan. The jeweler leased the area and unsuccessfully mined for more. He salted the area with inferior gems trying to attract investors to his Eagle Diamond Mining Company. (Internet Archive.)

HISTORIC ANIMALS. Eagle's terrain provided habitat for bears, wolves, elk, and buffalo. In the early 2000s six extinct eastern elk remains were discovered in a marl trap near Paradise Springs. There is limited evidence of buffalo in Eagle, but the open prairie would have been ideal habitat. It was reported that in the 1840s, pioneers Jonathan Betts and John Maul saw them in Eagle, and Betts shot one in Oconomowoc. (WDNR.)

NATIVE AMERICAN INFLUENCE. When the early settlers began to inhabit Waukesha County and Eagle in the early 1830s, they infrequently encountered Native Americans but regularly came across remnants and artifacts. This picture shows a stereotypical teepee of the plains Indians, not the wigwam or longhouse that the woodland Indians lived in. It is suspected that this teepee was a tourist attraction to draw people to the newly formed Eagle Springs resort.

Two

Town of Eagle

Eagle received its name in 1836 when three prospectors—Thomas Sugden, John Coats, and William Garton—came across a beautiful prairie where a large bald eagle was seen. Later that year, 13 settlers came to the area, settling at least three different areas. Ahira Hinkley, Henry Hinkley, and Ebenezer Thomas settled in the Palestine area, the latter building a blacksmith forge there. Andrew Schofield, James Bigelow, and Dr. Daniel Bigelow settled in Eagleville with the latter building a sawmill followed by a grist (flour) mill the following year. Thomas Sugden and Joseph Smart settled in Jericho, finding Charles Cox and his family living in a covered wagon. They were followed by William Sherman and Jonathan Parsons. It is unknown where Richard Whitehouse and Harrison Ward settled. During the early years of the Town of Eagle, each of these hamlets competed to become the metropolis of Eagle. In addition to their main industry they built schools, stores, and taverns to support the surrounding population and entice additional settlers.

The next year, Jerry Parsons built a hotel in Jericho on the road to Madison and the West, which was intended for oxen teams hauling large convoys of lead from Mineral Point to Milwaukee. There are two stories of how the area got its name, with the first being that Jerry Parsons had a motley crew helping in his hotel, and they were called "Jerry and Company." The second is that he hung a large sign for his business reading "Jerry Co."

Also in 1837, Daniel Melendy settled in the northwest corner of the town that would be known as Melendy's Prairie.

Until 1839, Eagle was part of Mukwonago and then became a part of Genesee until becoming an independent town on January 12, 1841.

Both Jericho and Eagleville received a post office in the mid-1840s. In 1848, a post office called Bullion was formed at an unknown place in Eagle and maintained that name until 1854. It is believed this was the earliest name of Jericho.

TORNADO DESTRUCTION. The destruction pictured resulted from a tornado that went through Eagle either on August 16, 1907, or April 24, 1914. The former was reported to have destroyed barns, homes, and machinery and killed cows and horses across the county. During the latter tornado, it was reported that the house, barn, machine shed, and chicken house of the Richard Bogie farm

in Eagle was reduced to kindling. Fortunately, there was no loss of life in either event. Although infrequent, numerous tornados have come through Eagle. In addition to the two mentioned here, documented tornados occurred in Eagle in 1861, 1895, 1933, and 2010.

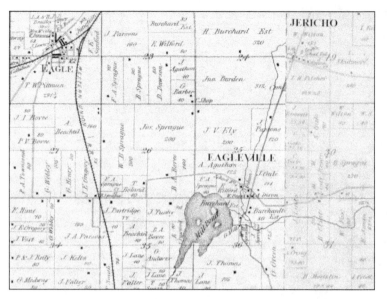

Jericho, 1873. Jericho had a blacksmith shop, a wagon shop, a harness shop, one or two stores, a creamery, a post office, a Baptist church, and a school. Comparing this 1873 map to the 1859 map at the front of this book, it can be seen that Jericho stagnated while Eagle Centre had prospered from the railway. (Author's collection.)

Walls of Jericho, Early 1900s. This photograph of County Trunk Highway (CTH) NN looks west across Jericho Creek. John Burden (1816–1883) settled here in the 1860s from England and farmed 312 acres of Section 24 in the southwest corner of Jericho. He enclosed his farm with masonry walls of limestone, which became known as the "Walls of Jericho." This farm is now Jericho Corners subdivision.

Jericho Blacksmith and Garage, c. 1925. William Michaelis (1894–1971) and son Donald Michaelis (1918–2009) are pictured at his garage. A wooden blacksmith shop was built by William Harris in 1868 and replaced with this stone one in the late 1880s. Donald would go on to become a co-pilot of B-24s in the South Pacific during World War II, flying 37 missions. The building still stands and is a garage of a private residence.

Jericho Creamery, c. 1910. Jericho cheese factory was in the northwest corner of Jericho and began in the 1870s and closed in the 1910s. In 1892, John Harris and Walter West owned the factory. Harris and his brother owned 12 cheese factories in Walworth and Waukesha Counties and were the sons of well-known cheesemaker James Bowie Harris from New York State. (EHS)

EAGLEVILLE LUMBER MILL. In the fall of 1836, Daniel Bigelow (1777–1863) established a small sawmill in the wilderness of Eagle. The earliest sawmills were very rudimentary since all the lumber to build them needed to be hauled in or sawed by hand. The sawmill was operated for at least 10 years and probably declined once the railroad was established. This is a representation of a simple lumber sawing operation. (WDNR.)

EAGLE GRIST MILL, C. 1915. The original mill was built in 1837 by Daniel Bigelow. It was sold and improved upon numerous times, with the biggest improvement occurring in 1844 by Andrew Scofield with the building of this structure. In 1875, Harvey Wambold purchased the mill and increased the dam size and thus the size of Eagle Springs Lake. The McCormick turbine that was used to produce electricity for the area was donated to Old World Wisconsin in 2013.

EAGLEVILLE EASTERN SPRINGS, C. 1910. Delia Sprague (1895–1963) is shown in front of the metal tubes used to raise the level of the spring water. This allowed Eagleville residents to get clean, fresh spring water before it flowed into the Mukwonago River. The springs were still in use until the 1950s. The area is currently covered with brush and owned by the Wisconsin Department of Natural Resources

EAGLE LAKE AVENUE, C. 1920. A car travels down Eagle Lake Avenue in front of Eagleville school. A portion of this road still retains that name in the Village of Mukwonago. In the mid-1900s, the county took over jurisdiction, naming it CTH NN. In 1967, Rainbow Springs Resort petitioned for a state trunk highway (STH), causing this road to become STH 99 by switching names with the parallel road one mile north. In 1999, it became CTH LO, honoring Lloyd Owens, the 1964–1984 Waukesha County Board chairman.

CLARK'S PARK, C. 1920. Pictured is Albert Charles Clark (1868–1927, right), Illinois state senator and president of the A.C. Clark Brass and Iron Manufacturing in Chicago. In 1912, he purchased about 34 acres on the northeast side of Eagle Springs Lake in Section 25 for $4,000. In 1924, he subdivided it into about 100 lots with various open areas for the residents, one of which was called Clark's Park. The baseball backstop in the background is still present.

WRESTLING MATCH, 1913. A large crowd watches a wrestling match at Clark's Park. Unfortunately, action photography was not very good in 1913, and the wrestlers are a blur. The crowd size is impressive; only part of it is seen here, yet it is nearly half of Eagle's 1910 population of 1,058. These people would have come from miles around, having to walk or ride a horse.

EAGLE SPRINGS LAKE CANOES, C. 1915. Canoes of the Eagle Springs Resort are positioned along the shore. Shown in the background are Highview peninsular (left), Toohill Island (center), and Traver's Island (right). Eagle Springs Lake is a 279-acre lake with a maximum depth of about eight feet, created by two dams holding the water back. There are five islands that have summer residences on them.

TOOHILL ISLAND. When the dam was built, the higher water level flooded the surrounding marsh, creating a lake and a series of islands. These islands are now filled with cottages and summer homes. Pictured on Toohill Island is a "clubhouse" built by J.A. Lins in the late 1800s. The house is still on the island, but the viewing tower is no longer there. It was used for entertaining guests and friends, and no connection to the golf course has been found.

EAGLE SPRINGS GOLF RESORT, POST 1921. The oldest golf resort in Wisconsin was founded in 1893 by William Tuohy on 200 acres in Section 35, which his Irish immigrant parents, John and Mary Tuohy, settled in 1866. It is currently owned by a sixth generation. On the left is the current clubhouse, which was the previous hotel's laundry building. Some of the cottages can be seen around the road. The hotel was located at about the center of the picture. (EHS.)

EAGLE SPRINGS HOTEL, 1912. The hotel was opened by William Tuohy (1870–1939) on June 18, 1910, to nearly 100 Chicagoans who came by a special railroad car and were driven from the Eagle train station via Ford automobiles. Hotel rates were $2 per day and $8–12 per week. Golf was 25¢ for 18 holes. The hotel was sold in 1921 by the heartbroken William after his daughter unexpectedly died at 21, and was torn down. In 1929, the golf course was reduced to nine holes due to the Depression.

SPRINGS OF EAGLE SPRINGS RESORT, C. 1920. This view of the springs and gazebo looks southeast from the Eagle Springs Hotel. The round concrete tubes protected the springs from filling in with dirt. The gazebos provided a shaded place to rest and drink fresh spring water before it flowed into the small pond and then Eagle Springs Lake.

EAGLE SPRINGS GAZEBO, 1910. From left to right, Mary Tuohy (1896–1986), Delia Sprague (1895–1963), Agnes Tuohy (1899–1920), and Isabelle Ely (1896–1956) stand in one of Eagle Springs Golf Resort's gazebos. Agnes and Isabelle hold onto a rope that holds a drinking ladle so people could get a drink of fresh, cold spring water.

MINNEHAHA SPRINGS. The first grant of the land currently known as Paradise Springs was from Pres. James Polk to William Robinson in 1844. Being poor farming ground, it was resold numerous times. Joseph Sprague and Marvin Bovee both owned it for a period. In the 1880s, J.A. Lins purchased it and called it Minnehaha Springs. Being a prominent businessman, he built a pavilion over the spring and allowed people to picnic and enjoy the springs as a goodwill gesture. (EHS.)

DAM AND TURBINE HOUSE, C. 1910. When Francis M. Nichols (1834–1916) acquired the property in the early 1900s, he built a water-driven turbine on the east side of the concrete dam. The turbine created electricity, giving him one of the first electrified homes in the area. Remnants of the turbine house can still be seen. Numerous sources mention L.D. Nichols, but F.M. Nichols is on the plat map and census records. (WDNR.)

PARADISE SPRINGS SWANS, 1920S. Louis Petit (1857–1932), a wealthy businessman and banker from Milwaukee, made extensive improvements to Paradise Springs. A 1956 newspaper article stated, "Petit added interest to his estate by placing, first white swans in his pool, then later black swans, but color tensions and riots arose, and the blacks had to go."

PARADISE SPRINGS SPRING HOUSE. The springhouse was built in the early 1930s by Louis Petit, who created the Eagle Rock Springs company to sell the spring water to spas, hotels, and health resorts. The springs at that time were measured at 200–600 gallons per hour. Springwater from this house was bottled and sold by various companies until the late 1960s. The copper dome was removed by the Department of Natural Resources in 1975 to prevent theft.

PARADISE SPRINGS HORSE TRACK, C. 1930S. Louis Petit used Paradise Springs for vacation and a business opportunity. A horse lover, he constructed a small racetrack in the 1920s where he could be seen exercising his favorite trotter. This picture shows the former driveway, which is now the walkway entrance to the Paradise Springs Nature Trail. (WDNR.)

PARADISE SPRINGS HORSE TRACK. Louis Petit's grandson Douglas Bournique (1919–1983) is shown jumping his horse. His sister Eugenie married August Pabst of the Pabst Brewing Company family and inherited the land when Petit passed in 1932. The track was abandoned, and the land was resold in 1936.

EAGLE LIME PRODUCTS, C. 1909. The lime company operated from 1909 to 1915 and produced 20 tons of marl per month. Marl is a carbonate-rich mud that was used for fertilizer and mortar and found in Eagle's marshes. The mill was in Ottawa and a railway was planned to ship dredged soil from Eagle to the mill, but it did not materialize. The coming of the automobile and synthetic fertilizers helped end that enterprise. (WDNR.)

MELENDY'S PRAIRIE. The northwest corner of Eagle has a prairie that extended into Jefferson County that was settled by Daniel Melendy (1810–1887) in 1837. The people of this area tended to associate more with Palmyra due to a large marsh separating it from Eagle. Melendy's Prairie had a small, dispersed community with a church, a blacksmith shop, a school, a creamery, and a few farms. (Author's collection.)

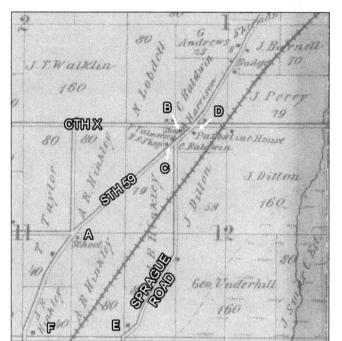

PALESTINE, 1859. Ahira Hinkley and Andrew Schofield were scouting the area for a place to settle when they reached a spring near what would later become Palestine. Hinkley cut his name into a tree, thus making the first land claim in the town on September 20, 1836. The Palestine population center is still noticeable at the intersection of County Highway X and Sprague Road, although STH 59 now bypasses it. The town had a school (A), a store (B), a blacksmith shop (C), and a tavern (D). (Author's collection.)

PALESTINE COBBLESTONE HOUSE. Upon settling, Ahira Hinkley built a 12-by-16-foot log house (E above) on his property. Around 1850, he built a cobblestone house, shown here (F). Ahira mortgaged his farm for $2,000 for a railroad bond with expectations of getting a train station in Palestine. When that did not happen, Palestine's potential faded into a footnote of history. (EHS.)

Three

EAGLE CENTRE

The competition between the population centers changed in 1851 when the southern branch of the Milwaukee & Mississippi Railroad was laid through the town of Eagle. Eagle Centre was placed at the intersection of Romeo Sprague's, Thomas Pitman's, and William Kline's properties. Kline donated three acres at the southeastern corner of his land for a depot. These three entrepreneurs subdivided their lands around the depot, thus creating Eagle Centre. This area quickly became the new population center of the town.

Although the details seem to be lost to time, one can imagine the deal that was struck to have the railroad put its depot there in lieu of Ahira Hinkley's offer. One theory is that since Pittman was a significant land speculator with large landholdings, he traded easements across his many miles of land for the depot being placed where he could best profit.

When selecting a name for the new population center, the group recommended calling it Pittman, but he declined the offer and suggested Eagle Centre, which it became. In 1880, Eagle Centre was claimed to be the third most important population center in the county. It had a large mill, two dry goods houses, two hardware stores, two clothing shops, three churches (Baptist, Methodist, and Catholic), four saloons, a butcher shop, a grocer, a harness shop, a hotel, a school, and a post office. One disadvantage of Eagle Centre was that its low-cost energy source of Eagle Springs was quite a distance from the railroads. Had the power source been near the railroad, Eagle would have most likely developed like the larger manufacturing towns of Burlington, Whitewater, Jefferson, and Fort Atkinson.

Due to differing opinions regarding the temperance movement between Eagle Centre and the Town of Eagle, in 1899, Eagle Centre was incorporated as the Village of Eagle to prevent its liquor establishments from being closed.

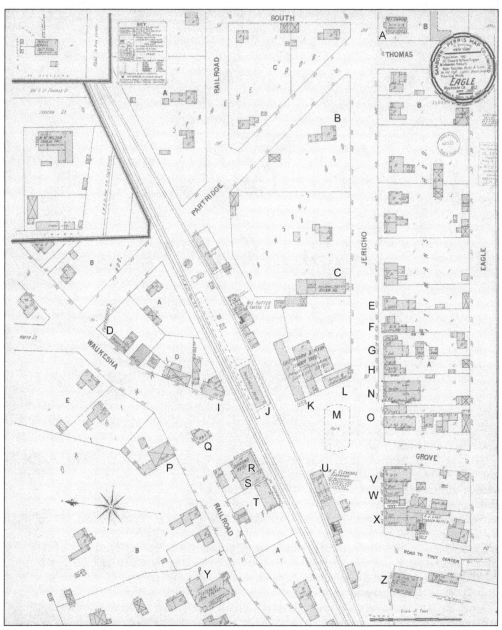

VILLAGE OF EAGLE MAP, 1906. Since many places have changed their names over the years as well as how they look, this map provides a common reference point for this chapter's photographs. Historically, P through T was called the "Hotel Block." E through O was the "Business Block," and V through X was the "Bank Block." Although many of the buildings had multiple shops or stores within them, a single letter is assigned for each building. (Library of Congress.)

EAGLE ELEVATOR, C. 1900. The elevator was used to store grain for the local farmers until it was needed or sold. It was built around 1880 and owned by Harvey Clemons (1847–1925) and Don Pardee (1881–1927). In 1923, it was sold to Bentley Dadmun (1878–1962) of Whitewater. In 1970, the village bought the mill for $70.14 (the amount of delinquent taxes plus interest) and tore it down. (EHS.)

CHICAGO, MILWAUKEE & ST. PAUL RAILROAD. A coal-fired train with a passenger car is parked in front of the hotels of Eagle. Many of the trains traveling this line were for passenger service since it was the main type of transportation between towns. It was also used for commuting, as an 1892 directory listed 14 people who worked in Eagle but resided outside of the town, typically in Waukesha.

PANORAMIC VIEW OF THE NORTH SIDE OF EAGLE, C. 1925. From left to right are Harvey Clemons Elevator (U), St. Theresa's Church (Y), Commercial Hotel (T), Saloon (S), Diamond Hotel (R), a hotel in the far background (P), Ihrig's boot and shoe manufacture (Q), a residence, the

passenger station (J), and a lumber company (K). There is a park in the foreground (M). (See map on page 32 for building locations.) While a lot has changed over the years, the hotels still look the same. (EHS.)

EAGLE DEPOT, 1912. The passenger depot was built in the 1890s to protect passengers from the elements as they waited for a train to travel to the neighboring towns. The railroad brought in coal, oil, and lumber and shipped livestock, cheese, milk, and grain to Milwaukee. From there it was shipped by boat to the East. Eagle's passenger service was discontinued in 1953 and the depot was razed in 1956.

PASSENGER STATION. In the left background is the J.A. Lins elevator, which had a 25-horsepower steam engine. It was bought by the Wisconsin Butter and Cheese Company and used as a creamery in the early 1900s. In the right background is the lumber yard. (Roxanne Raduechel-Butler.)

BRITTINGHAM & HIXON LUMBER COMPANY. The lumber company was started in 1891 as G.W. Yerkes and Co. In 1896, it became Brittingham & Hixon. The large fence was used as a screen to show movies on. Gerald Von Rueden was the store manager for 42 years. In the background from left to right are the millinery, confectionery (H), and hardware and dry goods stores (N).

NORTH SIDE OF MAIN STREET, C. 1906. Historically the furniture maker was also the town's undertaker since they built the caskets, which is why the store on the left (L) has signs for both. A small wind-operated water tower is between the store and the opera house (C). The town did not have underground water piping, so wells and small wind-driven water towers were spread around town for residents to get their water. (Roxanne Raduechel-Butler.)

FOURTH OF JULY, 1924. Roy Henderson (1889–1955), a Masonic leader from Whitewater, gives a patriotic speech at the bandstand in the village park (M). Without televisions or radios, the local entertainment was at the bandstand or dances at the next-door Masonic lodge. The bandstand was torn down in 1964.

EAGLE ALUMINUM DRIVE, 1941. Local Boy Scouts are shown with the aluminum they gathered to support the preparation for World War II. Although the United States had not entered the war yet, it had been raging for two years and America was supporting the Allies by building aluminum-dependent equipment such as planes. At the end of the Great Depression, Scout uniforms were a cost many families could not afford.

MASONIC LODGE, C. 1900. The Rob Morris Lodge was granted a charter in 1859 with seven members. In 1893, the Rob Morris Lodge Building and Mercantile Association erected this building as an amusement hall, Masonic lodge, and meeting place for the Eastern Star chapter (C). The first floor had a seating capacity of 350 people. (EHS.)

INSIDE THE MASONIC LODGE, 1907. This building was also used as an opera house, for movie screenings and Eagle Cornet Band performances, as a space for an acting troupe known as the Rotnour Players, and for fairs, as shown in this photograph. In 1938, the radio station WLS hosted a talent show here. It later became a handbag factory. It was remodeled in 1958 as an apartment building, which it remains today. (EHS.)

GROCERY STORE. Men pose on the wooden boardwalk in front of the drug store (left) and dry goods store. The dry goods store was built on the corner of Main street (Jericho) and Grove (O) around 1875 by Matthias Bovee's son Edward. Milton and Victoria Krestan purchased the store in 1944, and their family operated it until 2000. (EHS.)

VAN HOLTEN'S PICKLE FACTORY. Eagle's pickle factory was on the main street near the current fire department and moved into the creamery building when it closed in the 1930s. Cucumbers from area farms would be brought to the factory, sorted, and pickled in large vats about 15 feet high and 20 feet in diameter. It operated until the early 1950s supplying pickles to Milwaukee's Van Holten pickle company. (EHS.)

BUSINESS BLOCK, C. 1905 Although the store owners, names, and merchandise have changed through the years, this area has continued to be a retail location. The pictured horse carts lining the street indicate a busy shopping day. From front to back in 1906, the buildings are a dry goods and boot and shoe store (O), a drugstore, a hardware store, a dry goods store (N), and a confectionary (H). (EHS.)

MAIN STREET LOOKING WEST, C. 1920. By the time of this photograph, things had changed a bit, with the buildings being, from left to right, a combined barbershop, bakery, and post office (G). The next building was a combined millinery and confectionary (H), hardware and dry goods (N), and drugstore, boots and shoes, and dry goods (O). In the distance, the bank block and the mill can be seen. (EHS.)

MCWILLIAMS HARDWARE STORE, C. 1875. James McWilliams (1819–1894) and son Walter Hunt McWilliams (1847–1931), shown at right, operated the hardware store in Eagle in the late 1800s. This building is where the Eagle Public Market currently is. In the early 1890s, it is suspected of being remodeled and combined with the property next to it. This building was brick veneer and burned down in a fire in 1972. (Felicia McWilliams Froschmayer.)

SMART BROTHERS GARAGE, C. 1912. Brothers Edward (1872–1939) and Harry Smart (1876–1950) operated a garage in Eagle in the early 1900s in a building that was previously a blacksmith shop. As transportation changed from horses to cars, blacksmiths often changed to garages. The Smarts opened additional garages in Mukwonago, Burlington, and Elkhorn. From left to right are Art Silvernail, Max Sadenwasser, and Harry Smart. The building burned down in 1918.

BANK BLOCK, C. 1915. The four buildings at left above are also seen on the right below: from left to right are Jay W. Stead Furniture and Undertaking (V), Belling Bros Meat Market, a harness shop, Bank of Eagle and Eagle Telephone Co. (W), the Blue Ribbon Saloon, an autoist headquarters (X), and at far right above, a wagon shop. The furniture store was originally Charles Lins's hardware store. The meat market was started by brothers Edward and John Lins in 1864. Arthur Bellings purchased it in 1898 and operated it until growing competition from supermarkets and his age caused him to retire in 1963. The building held various shops over the years and is currently the restaurant Rustix. The bank and Blue Ribbon were rebuilt after burning down in a fire in 1929 and have remained those business types through the years. (Both, EHS.)

TRAIN CRASH, MAY 20, 1922. A westbound freight train with 16 cars derailed about three miles west of Eagle when a car containing oil left the track and ran alongside it for 300 feet. The 10 cars following the tank plunged down either side of the embankment. As can be seen here, there was quite a bit of interest from the locals to see the wreckage.

EAGLE TRAIN GRAVEL PIT, C. 1915. A steam engine is shown receiving water for its boilers. The 1914 Eagle map shows a spur and staging area just to the west of the village where gravel was dug out for track-bed creation and maintenance. The marsh imposed a significant obstacle that required extensive fill. Years later, a bulldozer sunk and was lost in the marsh when creating STH 59. The gravel pit is now overgrown within the Kettle Moraine Forest.

Four

LIFESTYLE

The lives and methods of how people lived and worked in the late 1800s and early 1900s have significantly changed over the years. Although these photographs are viewed from a modern perspective, many of them show the latest technology and work-saving machines that made lives significantly better at the time. For example, a 1920 truck hauling 100 gallons of milk at 20 miles per hour was a huge improvement over hitching up a team of horses to pull that same load at half the speed, although that truck is rudimentary compared to a modern 8,000-gallon milk truck traveling at 70 miles per hour.

While modern conveniences were not available to everyone in town at the same time, the general timeline of some of the biggest improvements to quality of life is as follows. The Eagle Telephone company was founded in 1902. The Ford Model T was introduced in 1908, leading to the transition from horse and buggy to affordable automobiles and all the changes that spurred from it. Harley Davidson motorcycles started becoming popular in the 1910s. The muddy, rough roads that the early "autoists" had to travel transitioned to gravel and then paved roads. Winter travel changed from pulling sleighs over the snow to plowed roads.

In 1922, the village of Eagle began to receive electricity. The Baker farm received it in 1932, but the Sprague farm did not receive it until 1936. With electricity came lights and indoor plumbing. Before then, it was windmills, hand pumps, lanterns, and trips to the privy. The heating of houses evolved from splitting and hauling wood logs to coal, then oil, and finally, natural gas and propane.

Compare how much people's lives changed with telephones, electricity, and automobiles back then with the modern-day introductions of the internet, mobile phones, and online shopping. One can imagine their great-great-grandfather saying, "I don't need one of those new-fangled telephones or automobiles; if I need to talk to someone, I'll visit them on my horse."

SPRAGUE FAMILY TRAVEL, C. 1910. From left to right, Theodore, Frances, Delia, Jesse, unidentified, Mary (née Brady), and Alice Sprague are shown on or around a carriage. It is unknown if they were just going for a ride or somewhere specific, like church. Eagle Centre was only two miles away, but it took over an hour to harness, hitch, and travel to the village.

WINTER TRAVEL, C. 1910. Theodore and Fanny Sprague ride a sleigh on the Sprague farm. Winter roads—if they could be called roads—were not plowed, and therefore, winter travel consisted of a horse trudging through the snow, pulling a sleigh.

PHAETON CARRIAGE AND HORSE, C. 1920. A trotting horse is pulling Vinton Sherman (1891–1985) in a phaeton carriage. Sherman went on to operate the grocery store in Eagle with his wife, Eulalia, for 47 years until 1968. He also was a volunteer firefighter and a member of the Lions Club and the village board. These carriages were considered quite fast at the time, at 10 to 15 miles per hour.

COW POWER, C. 1910. An unknown boy sits on a simple cart being pulled by a young steer. This was not a typical method of transportation and may have been more for fun or general travel around the farm.

EAGLEVILLE UPHILL BIKE GANG, C. 1910. Eagleville was separated by a large hill where families were called either the "Uphills" or "Downhills." The children of the Uphill families who lived around Sprague Road and LO are showing off their bicycles. From left to right are Sidney Sprague, Katherine Bovee, Delia Sprague, Isabelle Ely, Chester Pratt, and James Bovee.

BIKE TRAVEL, LATE 1910S. Agnes Tuohy (left) and Frances Bovee pose for a photograph with their bicycles. The early 1900s saw an increase in the popularity of bicycles with the invention of the rear chain drive and the pneumatic tire. They were faster than walking and did not require having, nor hitching up, a horse. As can be seen here, the roads were still not paved.

MOTOR BIKES, C. 1915. From left to right are Roy Wambold (grandson of Harvey, 1891–1975), unidentified, and brothers John (1895–1978) and William Colwell (1894–1982) on their 1913 9B Harley Davidson motorbikes. Harley Davidson was founded in 1903 with production volumes being sufficient in the 1910s for many people to be able to purchase them.

HARLEY DAVIDSON WITH SIDECAR, C. 1915. This photograph is labeled Bull and Ted Michaelis, but they cannot be found in historical records. Harley's 61-cubic-inch V-twin design with 11 horsepower was powerful enough to pull a sidecar and passenger. The US Postal Service used sidecars for Rural Free Delivery, and they became popular during World War I. Seven out of ten Harleys included a sidecar, and 16,000 combinations were sold by 1919.

POSING WITH AN AUTOMOBILE, 1910. From left to right, Mary Tuohy, Delia Sprague, Agnes Tuohy, Isabelle Ely, and an unidentified boy pose with a 1910s Ford touring car at Eagle Springs. The car was used to transport patrons the three-and-a-half miles between the train station and Eagle Springs resort.

COUNTRY DRIVE, 1911. Unidentified drivers and passengers are visiting the Sprague family, who pose around the cars. The car on the left is a Ford Model T Runabout and the one on the right is a Hudson right-hand-drive Model 20. Both cars were made in Michigan. Hudson merged with Nash, a Kenosha car manufacturer, to become the American Motors Corporation in 1954 and ultimately Chrysler in 1987.

MILK TRUCK. Lizzie Rockteacher (1898–1957) is shown driving an early 1900s Ford Model T truck used as a milk truck in front of the Sprague Farm. Trucks were expensive but were quite an improvement over the horse and cart. Often, to distribute cost, one person would have a milk route picking up the various farmers' milk, freeing them up to increase their farm size and milk more cows.

WINTER TRAVEL, 1936–1937. This image of Sprague Road looks north within Section 24. No residence was shown at that location on the 1859 map. The winter of 1936–1937 received heavy snowstorms followed by bitter cold and high winds. Newspapers reported that Chicago ran out of milk and coal, and shortages in Southern Wisconsin occurred due to trains being stuck in the snow.

CUTTING ICE ON EAGLE SPRINGS LAKE, JANUARY 27, 1912. Before mechanical refrigeration, ice was cut and stored to be used to cool food through the summer. Once the lake froze to at least a foot deep, the ice would be cut into blocks with large saws, as shown here. These floating blocks would then be pushed toward a waiting wagon.

LOADING ICE BLOCKS, 1912. Ice blocks were cut to various sizes and could weigh between 300 and 600 pounds. Blocks were cut as large as possible to minimize the amount of work to cut them as well as to slow the melting rate by reducing the surface area.

HAULING ICE, 1912. This is a bird's-eye view of ice being removed from Eagle Springs Lake. After being cut and loaded, the horses would haul the ice to various icehouses, where they were unloaded and covered with insulating material such as marsh hay, corn stalks, or wood shavings. The 1906 Eagle Centre fire map shows six ice houses in the village and four around Eagle Springs.

ICE CHEST. Jesse Sprague's ice chest, now owned by the author, is pictured here. This is an insulated box that stored food similar to a modern-day refrigerator except it used ice to keep food cold. The ice would go in the lower left section and, as it melted, would drain out through a hose at the bottom. (Author's collection.)

WOOD LOADING. Jesse Sprague and an unidentified person sit on the load of a horse-drawn sleigh. The logs would be transported to the house for storage until they were able to be sawn. The Sprague farm had about 50 acres of wooded pasture about a half mile from the house.

STACKING WOOD TO DRY. Jesse Sprague poses with stacked logs near the farm. The logs were stacked vertically to reduce ground contact, helping them dry and decrease rotting. Many piles of wood would be prepared so when a portable saw was available, a large amount could be cut at once.

SAWING LOGS, C. 1910. A self-powered portable saw is being used to cut logs to a manageable length so they can be split. This is usually called bucking and is done today with a chain saw. Notice the limited guards and safety mechanisms.

WOODPILE, 1910. Sidney Sprague is posing with his large pile of split wood in front of the Sprague barn. After the logs were sawed to length, they would need to be split to allow them to dry and burn better. As seen here, large amounts of wood needed to be cut, hauled, and split for heating and cooking each year.

LAUNDRY DAY, C. 1910. Alice (left, 1886–1972) and Frances Sprague (1852–1916) are shown doing laundry on the Sprague farm. During the heat of summer, the breeze and coolness of a shade tree were quite nice compared to a house without air conditioning. Also, the laundry was closer to the water handpump, seen at upper right.

MILK CAN CLEANING, 1911. Alice Sprague cleans the milk cans that had returned from the creamery. Although the relation of cleanliness to health was still being discovered, many farmers followed hygienic methods. Wisconsin did not require pasteurization until the 1950s.

PEELING POTATOES. Frances (left) and Katherine Bovee peel potatoes. Potatoes were a mainstay of the farmer's diet, typically being served at each meal because of their high-calorie content and ease of growing and storing.

HUSKING HICKORY NUTS. Hickory nuts were regularly collected in the fall, when the husks were removed from the nuts to dry. The nuts would later be cracked, removing the meat for baking and other treats. From left to right are Delia Sprague, Fanny Sprague (back), Alice Sprague (front), and Lillian Martin.

SHEEP SHEARER. Carl Anderson (1861–1932) of Walworth County is shown with a powered, mechanical shearer. As an early case of outsourcing of labor, he traveled from farm to farm shearing sheep. An experienced shearer and his equipment were efficient enough to justify their cost and helped increase farmers' profitability.

CARPENTER WITH TOOLS. This photograph is labeled "Dutch" Thomas, who could not be found in records. He is believed to be Benjamin Franklin Thomas (1859–1942), the son of original settler Ebenezer Thomas. He is shown with the rudimentary hand tools that were used for carpentry and building houses.

CHILDREN ON A FENCE, C. 1920. Unidentified children sit on a roll of fence that was being put up. The early 20th century was a transition phase from mostly home-sewn clothes to purchased clothes; however, the Great Depression of the 1930s and World War II of the 1940s slowed this transition due to reduced income and rationing.

GIRLS IN DRESSES. It was common for girls to regularly wear dresses. They were easy to make and allowed for growth. In the early 20th century, many dresses were made from upcycled feed or flour sacks. Manufacturers discovered people were buying their brands for the bags, so they began making the bags out of nicer cotton and adding patterns to help boost sales.

STREETCAR LINE. This is a double-exposure photograph that Sidney Sprague created of a streetcar line and the main street of Eagle. Eagle never had a streetcar line. Double exposure was a technique where two photographs would be taken on the same film creating various creative photographs. It was quite an impressive feat to superimpose the track, car, and overhead lines onto Main Street. The differences between the shadows of the buildings and trees and the lack of them on the streetcar give it away.

TWO-PERSON CARD GAME. This double-exposure photograph of the same two people makes it look like a four-person card game. Don Marty is in the background, with an unidentified person in the foreground.

Five

FARM LIFE

Farming was historically the main occupation in Eagle, with 167 farms in 1859. The population centers grew to support local agriculture and their success was based on the success of the farms. Farmers would bring their produce to Eagle Centre to be shipped to the larger cities of Milwaukee and Chicago or have it processed into cheese, butter, or flour.

The earliest settlers mainly grew cereal grains and raised sheep, but they often diversified their farms to protect themselves from failure. The area's sheep industry focused on Spanish Merino sheep, which were said to provide the best fleeces. The wool market exploded in profitability during the Civil War due to the inability to get cotton from the South. Unfortunately, after the Civil War, the wool market steadily declined with the return of cotton and the beginning of synthetic fibers. This caused Eagle to transition over time to the dairy industry and corn to provide food for the cows. With the building of creameries, milk was converted to more valuable and longer-lasting butter and cheese.

While these pictures are mainly of the Sprague farm, it can be assumed that they are representative of the many other farms in the area. The advantage of highlighting a single farm in detail shows the continual progression and changes through time to adapt to market conditions and improvements in technology. However, each farm progressed at its own pace and had its own successes and failures.

Many of the farms on the northern and western sides of Eagle were bought by the state and torn down in the 1960s, returning those lands to nature within the Southern Kettle Moraine State Forest. Southern portions of Eagle have been subdivided into smaller horse estates, and many farms in the eastern portions have been torn down for housing developments. Only a few historic farms still exist, and most of them are in various stages of decay.

TOWNS.	NUMBER OF BUSHELS.										No. Acres Harvested for Seed.		Number of Pounds.				
	Wheat.	Corn.	Oats.	Barley.	Rye.	Potatoes.	Root Crops.	Cranberries.	Apples.	Clover Seed.	Timothy S'd.	Clover.	Timothy.	Flax.	Hops.	Tobacco.	Grapes.	Butter.	Cheese.
Eagle	19951	71507	41391		13626	6021	2545	37	1360	283		177	22		1400	4500	293300	31240	54230

TOWNS.	NUMBER OF ACRES.								APPLE ORCHARDS.							MILCH COWS.
	Wheat.	Corn.	Oats.	Barley.	Rye.	Potatoes.	Root Crops.	Cranberries.	No of Acres.	No of Bearing Trees.	Flax.	Hops.	Tobacco.	Grasses.	Growing Timber.	Number.	Value.
Eagle	1649	2670	1443	11	888	118	14	25	177	7181	3	4	3	2905	3590	684	11540

TOWNS.	HORSES.		NEAT CATTLE.		MULES AND ASSES.		SHEEP AND LAMBS.		SWINE.		WAGONS, CARRIAGES AND SLEIGHS.		WATCHES.		PIANOS AND MELODEONS.		BANK STOCK.	
	Number.	Value.	Number.	Value.	Number.	Value.	Number.	Value.	Number.	Value.	Number.	Value.	Number.	Value.	Number.	Value.	Number.	Value.
Eagle	459	25181	1153	16741	4	135	5782	12432	1009	2372	425	8241	41	606	33	1575		

EAGLE AGRICULTURE PRODUCTION, 1878–1879. The top chart shows how much of each crop was grown in 1878. The middle chart shows the number of acres planted in 1879, and the bottom chart shows the inventory of animals and personal property. It is interesting to note how many cranberries, hops, tobacco, grapes, and apples were grown in Eagle. (University of Wisconsin–Madison.)

PLOWING, C. 1915. Edwin Ely (right) and an unidentified person are plowing a small field. The horse would pull the plow while Ely directed it. Plowing fields prepared the seedbed by turning the soil over and killing the weeds. It was unusual for someone to be riding the horse while plowing. Horses were used after teams of oxen usually "sod busted" the virgin prairie grass.

DISCING, C. 1920. An unidentified person is discing the Eagle prairie with a single gang disc. The disc would level and loosen the soil to prepare the seedbed for good soil-to-seed contact during planting. While there are now a lot more trees in Eagle, it can be seen here how the prairie once stretched as far as one could see.

TALL CORN, C. 1910. Jesse Sprague (1888–1971) stands in front of some very tall corn. The rich, well-drained soil of the prairie produced some excellent crops when it received ideal weather and proper care of the soil with crop rotation and animal waste fertilizer.

CUTTING OATS, LATE 1920S. Jesse Sprague and his children are pictured on the binder-reaper cutting oats; from left to right are Gerald, Jesse, Joseph, and June. On the ground are the children of neighbor Charles Cruver (1874–1963). Jesse had 200 acres, with about 150 tillable and 50 as pastured woods. In the left background is Red Brae hill.

DRYING WHEAT. People load grain bundles onto wagons on Jesse Sprague's portion of the Eagle Prairie, southeast of Eagle Centre. The grain would be cut and left to dry on the prairie and then brought to the barn, where the grain would be separated from the chaff. St. Theresa's church spire is barely visible in the right background above the tree line.

CUTTING CORN, C. 1905. Theodore Sprague (1848–1924), Jesse's father, uses a binder to cut corn. The binder cut the corn and bundled the stalks in bundles about a foot in diameter. The discharge chute unloaded the bundles in a pile where they would be stood upright for the corn and stalks to dry. The strings on the horses are fly netting to prevent biting flies from landing on the horses.

RIDING THE EMPTY WAGONS, 1944. Jesse Sprague (right) drives the wagon with unidentified people to get another load. Although tractors were becoming more prevalent at this time, there were still too few of them, and being slow, they were typically used for stationary tasks.

WILSON'S FARM. Unidentified people thresh grains at the Wilson farm in Mukwonago. The thresher and steam engine were expensive pieces of equipment that single farms rarely could afford on their own. They were usually purchased by a cooperative, a traveling business, or the local government to increase the agriculture prospects of the area and thus tax revenue.

GRAIN WAGON. Workers take a break on the "fruits of their labor." The separated grain was bagged, put on wagons, and taken to Eagleville or Eagle's mills. Some of it would be exported out of town, some ground into flour, and some used as feed for local animals.

THRESHING BREAK, C. 1915. The guys take a break from threshing in the shade of a tree while Alice (front) and Delia Sprague provide them water. As can be seen, harvesting was a manpower-intensive job where neighbors and friends helped each other out in return for help with their crops.

HUSKING CORN. Jesse Sprague (left) and an unidentified person husk corn. The corn stalks were cut and stacked in corn shocks to dry, as seen in the background. The outer husk was removed to further dry the corn for storage to feed to the animals throughout the year. Field corn that is fed to animals is different from sweet corn, which people tend to be more familiar with.

STEAM ENGINE SILAGE PRODUCTION. The steam engine on the left powered a feed cutter that would chop and blow the corn stalks into the top of the silo. The weight of the silage would compress the air out, creating an anaerobic fermentation that would preserve the wet silage. The silage provided food with more nutrition than just cob corn and hay to provide the cows with food through the winter.

WINTERTIME TRANSPORTATION OF MILK, C. 1910. Oren Sprague (1892–1914) gets ready to take milk to the local creamery. The Sprague farm was called "Surprise Farm" due to a ridgeline that ran through it. The farm did not look very big from the road, but people were surprised once they crossed over the ridge and could see the expansive Eagle Prairie.

MILK WAGON WITH SKIS, C. 1915 Hired hands load a skied wagon for winter transport from the Sprague farm to the creamery. The Sprague farm had the advantage of being about two miles from both the Eagle and Jericho creameries, so it could deliver to whichever was paying better. Roads were not plowed, so a wagon with skis was critical for winter transportation.

MANURE SPREADER. An unidentified person on a manure spreader prepares to take a load to the fields. The manure was put on the fields to provide valuable nutrients for the next year's crops. The manure would be shoveled or forked into the spreader, where a series of ground-driven chains and gears would then unload it in the field.

SPRAGUE-BOVEE POND, 1910. Cows are getting a drink of water from a pond that is shared between the Sprague and Bovee farms. Eagle is filled with small ponds that were created by the melting of chunks of ice during the glacial period called kettles. Pioneers often searched for these and settled near them to provide water for their animals.

JESSE SPRAGUE COW YARD, C. 1930S. Holstein cows are seen in the cow yard. Holstein cows produced significantly more milk than other breeds. Over the years, Jesse Sprague changed between Ayrshire, Jersey, Holstein, and Guernsey breeds. Each breed provided different advantages such as milk volume, quality, and butterfat content for making cheese and butter.

SHEEP IN PASTURE, 1910. Sheep are shown grazing on the Sprague farm. An old-fashioned split rail fence was used to keep the sheep in. Split-rail fence was an inexpensive way to keep animals fenced in with an available forest but was labor-intensive to make and upkeep. Today, the Eagles Aire and Westwind Subdivisions are in the background of this location.

SHEEP FEEDING, C. 1910. Jesse Sprague is feeding his sheep on his farm. In 1878, there were 5,782 sheep in the town. Growing sheep for meat and wool was quite profitable but slowly declined through the years. The decline was exacerbated by the invention of synthetic fibers for clothing and Americans switching to eating more beef.

PIGS. A mother sow feeds her large litter of piglets. While pigs were not the typical income maker for farms in Eagle, it was common for farmers to have them. Being natural foragers, they were easy to raise and required minimal support. In addition to being used for food, they were valuable for lard, which was used for cooking and baking.

CHICKEN FEEDING, C. 1910. Delia Sprague feeds the farm's chickens. Chickens provided eggs and meat for food as well as additional income for the family. Chickens are natural foragers of insects, but they are still provided grain to generate additional growth. Chickens are one of the most efficient animals at converting food to meat, and just like today, are an inexpensive meat source.

GEESE FEEDING. An unknown person is shown feeding geese. Geese were not as common as other animals on the farm but were an additional income source by providing the stereotypical "Christmas goose." They were also natural alarms, making quite a bit of noise if a predator was around.

SPRAGUE TURKEYS, C. 1930. June Sprague (1922–2020) is shown with turkeys being raised for Thanksgiving. During the Great Depression, farmers diversified with alternative ways to make a bit of money as well as ensure sufficient food. Sprague descendants continued to grow small quantities of fresh free-range turkeys for Thanksgiving until the early 2000s.

WILSON'S BARN. Here is a very clean barn in Mukwonago. Cows would be positioned between the rails with their heads in the stanchions to be milked. The cows would be fed on the outside lanes, and manure would fall into the inside gutters. Hay was stored in the loft above and dropped through small chutes. The small pens in the left background held the calves.

SPRAGUE'S BARN, C. 1950. Jesse Sprague (right) is pictured with unidentified individuals in his barn. The wooden stanchions used for holding the cows for milking were built perpendicular to the barn. Newer barns placed the stanchions parallel with the barn so the barn-cleaning conveyor would operate in a loop.

SHADYBROOK FARM, 1910s. Franz Baierl (1862–1943), wife Katherine (1867–?), sons Joseph (1898–1984), and George (1903–1989) are pictured on their farm at the southwest corner of Jericho. The wall in the photograph is a portion of the "Walls of Jericho." In 1969, the farm became the Red Brae Farm when brothers Edgar and Andy Armbruster began operating it. In 1994, the farm was torn down and became Jericho Corners subdivision.

ELDERWOOD TURKEY FARM. Father Roy (1882–1963) and Donald Burton (1907–1981) raised up to 5,000 turkeys a year for Thanksgiving from the late 1930s until the late 1970s in Section 6 in the northwest corner of Eagle. The house and barn are still there, but the turkey pens are gone. (Ryan Hajewski.)

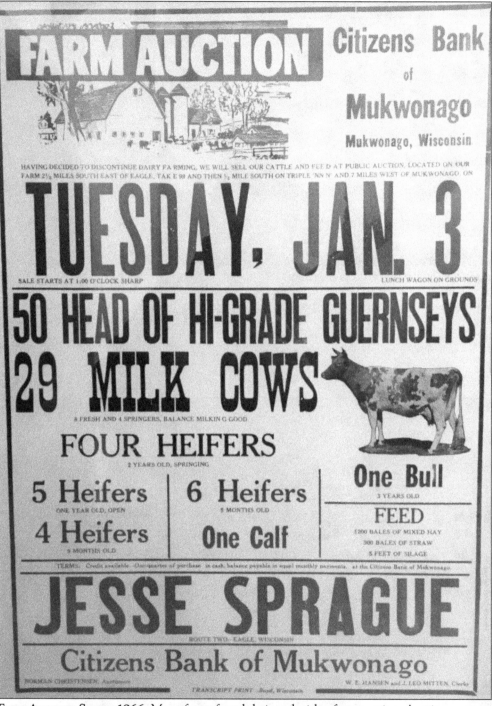

Farm Auction Sheet, 1966. Many farms found their end with a farm auction. Auctions were as much a social event as a sale, with neighbors coming to catch up with each other. The year 1966, the last time cows were on the Sprague farm, was near the beginning of declining dairy farms in Eagle. As fast as dairy farming replaced sheep farming, dairy farming itself disappeared in Eagle. Only the Grotjan Dairy and the Dempsey Farm, both in the northwest corner, still milk in Eagle.

Six

RECREATION

Although life was harder and work and daily activities like cooking and doing laundry required significantly more time, people still found free time to enjoy various activities in Eagle. With travel being slower and more difficult, most recreation was nearby. Old newspapers regularly include articles about people's travels that a modern person would consider trivial, such as family members visiting from Waukesha only 15 miles away.

People owned larger properties, which could serve dual purposes for recreation. Here, they picnicked, played sports, and hunted. Sidney Sprague loved playing croquet and built two courts where he regularly invited people over to play games. Eagle Springs Lake provided both summer and winter recreation with swimming, fishing, boating, and sailing. Resorts existed at Paradise Springs and Eagle Springs but tended to cater to richer tourists from the cities. As the town's density grew, common spaces were needed such as the Village Park and Clark's Park created by Illinois state senator A.C. Clark. Clark's Park required a fee to use and is now within a homeowner's association. Taverns were opened for people to gather and play cards, darts, or pool. Live music and dances were held at the Masonic Hall.

Many of these activities continue but some have changed or been reduced. The large farms have been subdivided into smaller properties, creating the need for parks for recreation spaces. The Ice Age Trail provides hiking and hunting opportunities. Many of the hours that were once spent outside have now moved indoors. The towns no longer compete against each other in sports, unless one counts school teams. Granted, the baseball diamonds are much nicer, with no trees growing in the middle and no manure to dodge.

CARRY ME AISY. Jim (left) and Benedict Bovee pose with Jesse Sprague's rowboat. The boat's name came from a historical saying that meant "easy-going" or "lazy." A family story stated that Jesse was called this when he had a batch of milk rejected because of a fly in one of the cans. He picked the fly out saying, "What does it matter if I pick out the fly or if they do?" and returned the batch of milk to the creamery the next day.

BOATING ON THE SPRAGUE-BOVEE POND, C. 1910. From left to right, James Bovee, Delia Sprague, Francis Bovee, Bovee's aunt Frances Robinson, and Katherine Bovee boat on the Sprague/Bovee pond. Jim, Francis, and Katherine were siblings and Delia was a second cousin. The Spragues and Bovees have been neighbors in Section 26 for six generations.

DAM SWIMMING AREA. Numerous people of the local community are shown enjoying a day out with a few people swimming by the Harvey Wambold Dam. A rudimentary wooden bridge previously went over the dam but is now the paved Wambold Road. The bridge over the dam is the only access to the people who live on the other side of the outlet.

SWIMMING, C. 1910. A group of Eagleville boys pose for a photograph. The swimmers are, from bottom to top, (left column) Bill Machold and James Bovee; (middle) Ben Bovee, Jack Roberts, Oren Sprague, and Don Marty; (right) unidentified, Jesse Sprague, and Ed Ketter. Swimming was a popular activity in Eagle Springs during the hot summers.

EAGLE BASEBALL TEAM. At far left in the first row is Don Marty (wearing the dark sweater), but no other details are known of this photograph. The players wear the uniform of Eagle's baseball team. It is assumed that the men with ties were coaches.

NORTH PRAIRIE BASEBALL TEAM, C. 1910. Shown is the North Prairie baseball team with a person from Ottawa. He may have been a substitute to get a full team of nine. Jesse Sprague is in the back row at center.

CLARK'S PARK BASEBALL TEAM, C. 1915. No details were preserved with this photograph. Although, interestingly, Clark's Park had its own team. It is possible that A.C. Clark sponsored the team to make it the Clark's Park team rather than the Eagleville team. Jesse Sprague is in the second row, second from left.

SILVER LEAGUE BASEBALL. These players are, from left to right, (first row) Frank Breidenbach, Don Marty, Dean Jones, Jack Lidicker, and Louis Sasso; (second row) two unidentified, Babe Markham, unidentified, Anton Steinhoff, Carl Belling, Ray Alpress, and Otto Marquardt. Most of them look like they came to play right from working on the farm.

CLARK'S PARK BASEBALL, 1915. Baseball is being played at Clark's Park in Eagleville. At this time, baseball was in its infancy, and without television, local games were often the only way for people to see a game. It is interesting that horses are freely grazing in the outfield; also, note the tree in left field. Currently, this is the open area behind Eagleville school. The tracks in the foreground became Lower Clark Park Road.

CLARK'S PARKS VIEWING STANDS, C. 1915. This is an opposite perspective of the photograph above. The hill was natural seating for spectators to watch the games. These games would be a social event for people to meet up with neighbors and friends. The hill is currently covered with trees.

GOLF. Golf was another popular activity within Eagle with the Eagle Springs Golf Course. It was originally an 18-hole course but decreased to nine during the Great Depression. In the 1960s, another golf course, Rainbow Springs, opened just down the road in Mukwonago. It closed in 2010, and the land was returned to nature and is managed by WDNR.

MARY AND AGNES TUOHY GOLFING, C. 1915. Mary and Agnes were the third generation of Eagle Springs golf resort. Eagle Springs is the oldest family-owned nine-hole golf course in Wisconsin and is currently owned by the sixth generation. It was ranked the 23rd best nine-hole golf course in the world by *Golf Magazine* in 2020.

DOG POWER. An unidentified person is shown on a sled being pulled by a dog for some fun. This was not a common method of transportation in Eagle.

HORSE SLEDDING, C. 1910. People use a horse to pull a sled for some fun on the Sprague Farm. Leisure time looked a little different in the time of horses. Now, people tie ropes to all-terrain vehicles or automobiles.

ICE SAILING, C. 1910. From left to right, Chester Pratt, unidentified, Jesse Sprague, and James Bovee pose for a photograph on Jesse Sprague's iceboat on Eagle Springs Lake. Ice sailing was a popular activity in the wintertime with Jesse Sprague and his friends. Due to low drag, iceboats could reach impressive speeds. The world speed record was set at 143 miles per hour in 1938 on Lake Winnebago, Wisconsin.

ICE SKATING. A family skates on a frozen snowmelt pond that is covering a road. Ice skating was also done on Eagle Springs Lake, but a nearby frozen pond was much easier to get to. The road's guard rails also made a nice bench to sit on.

Cow Pasture Catch, c. 1915. People play some kind of game in the Sprague cow pasture. Farmers used as much of their land as possible and did not have large lawns like people do now. Growing up in the 1980s, children still played baseball in cow pastures during family celebrations in Eagle—navigating around cowpies just added an extra challenge.

Merry-Go-Round, c. 1930. June Sprague, in the front, looks at the camera, and unidentified kids play on a historic merry-go-round at Eagleville School. Eagleville was a single-room schoolhouse, so all the grades learned and played together. This is what recess looked like almost 100 years ago.

SHADE TREE PICNIC. People enjoy an outdoor picnic. With the lack of electricity and thus air conditioning, eating outside was popular during the heat of summer.

POOL. Eagle Centre, Eagleville, Paradise Springs, and Jericho all historically had saloons or taverns, and this could be any one of them. The taverns have always been one of the main social locations for people, where they could get food and drink, play games, and catch up with friends and neighbors on the latest news and gossip. Today, only the Village of Eagle and Eagleville still have bars.

CHECKERS, C. 1920. Theodore Sprague (left) plays checkers against an unidentified person. Simple games like checkers and cards were common leisure activities with friends and family.

READING, 1910. Reading was another popular way to pass the time, as can be seen by Delia Sprague sitting by the stove. Interestingly, the lantern is lit, but there is enough daylight to take the photograph and cast shadows. Flash photography did not become prevalent until the late 1920s. *Rector of St. Mark's and Rosamond* is a Victorian romance novel published in 1874.

CROQUET COURT, C. 1935. From left to right, Gerald Von Rueden (1913–2003), Robert Cruver (1913–1973), Richard Gibson (1905–1978), and Sidney Sprague (1890–1957) pose for a photograph on one of Sidney's two croquet courts at his house on Sprague Road. He regularly hosted games with various friends and neighbors and was known for his impeccable maintenance of the courts. The courts are now gone.

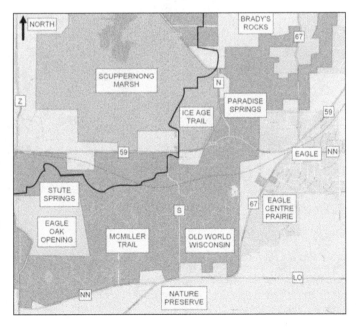

KETTLE MORAINE STATE FOREST. In 1961, Wisconsin governor Gaylord Nelson began a 10-year, $50 million Outdoor Recreation Acquisition Program. The program bought privately owned lands and preserved them as wildlife and recreation areas with a penny-a-pack tax on cigarettes and was the first program of its kind in the nation. Many farms in Eagle were purchased through this program and were reverted to nature creating numerous trails, including a portion of the Ice Age Trail. (Author's collection.)

SKUNK HUNTING. Unidentified people show off their hunting yields. On the top row are skunk hides; the fur was quite popular at various times, being warm, durable, and inexpensive. The bottom row is mostly muskrats, which provide durable fur and, being a water animal, have some natural water repellency. Also shown are a few rabbits, ducks, and deer antlers.

KIDS HUNTING. Kids show off their guns in preparation for a day of hunting. Hunting was a family affair that the parents and grandparents taught the children. Formal hunter education did not start in Wisconsin until 1967.

HISTORIC TRAP SHOOTING. People participate in trap shooting at an unknown location. Few details of trap shooting exist in Eagle until the opening of the McMiller sports complex. It is assumed that this picture was taken at Clark's Park. Trap shooting was done for fun as well as practice for hitting a moving target. The Town of Eagle banned target practice in 2017, even on private properties large enough for people to hunt on.

NORTHERN PIKES. Fish are hung up after a successful day of fishing on Eagle Springs Lake. The lake is still popular for both summer and winter fishing. Local farmers tended to ice fish more since they had less work in the winter. As the town's population grew and fishing pressure increased, the daily bag limit has decreased and is currently two northern pikes.

DUCK AND RABBIT SEASON, C. 1920. Jesse Sprague (left) and his second cousin and neighbor James Bovee show off the results of a successful day of hunting. This photograph also answers the age-old question; back then, it was both rabbit *and* duck season. The Spragues and Bovees have been neighbors since 1855, and their descendants still hunt together. An interesting anecdote is that although deer hunting is now quite popular in Eagle, Jesse never shot a deer. During the early 1900s, deer were over-harvested from unregulated hunting for their hides for the leather industry. Deer did not return to southern Wisconsin until the mid-1900s, and deer hunting was closed in Waukesha County between 1906 and 1954. Although the Wisconsin Department of Natural Resources allowed rifle hunting statewide in 2013, with research showing that rifles posed no greater risk than shotguns even in populated areas, the Town of Eagle still banned rifle hunting.

Seven
CIVIC LIFE

With the growth of the town came civic responsibilities to its citizens. Eagle became a town in 1841, and the village was incorporated in 1899. The local government's original primary responsibilities only included elections, property tax assessments, dispute resolution, and law enforcement, which was done by the supervisors.

Due to the limited scope of the local government, residents worked together for the institutions and services they desired. Individuals donated money and time, formed groups, and solicited the support of local businesses to support popular endeavors. Schools and churches were created when a group of neighbors worked together, donating land, materials, and knowledge to build and teach their children. This progressed to the town collecting school taxes to support the districts with full-time teachers.

Waukesha County took care of the main county roads, and the town paid farmers to take care of the local roads since they did not have a roads department.

The village's first newspaper was the *Eagle Quill* in 1880, but it also had the *Eagle News*, *Eagle Sun*, *Eagle Town Crier*, and *Zeitung* through the years. The first library was created in a section of a store on Main Street in 1905. The fire department started as an all-volunteer service in 1927. The 31-acre village park was created in 1946. The first chief of police of the Village of Eagle was in 1947. When America needed volunteers to support its wars, Eagle's citizens answered the call. When the veterans returned, the community supported them with the American Legion and the Ladies Auxiliary Legion. The Village of Eagle did not create a public water system until 1951, which led to the infamous smiley-face water tower.

Medical services were provided by various doctors supporting the community by making house calls as well as conducting appointments in their own houses until the first clinic was built in 1954.

Other charity groups included chapters of Eagle Lioness, Masonic Lodge, International Organization of Odd Fellows, and International Organization of Good Templars, as well as the unique organizations of the Eagle Advancement Association, Eagle Business Association, parent-teacher organizations, and various other groups. All these groups helped build Eagle into the town and village they are today.

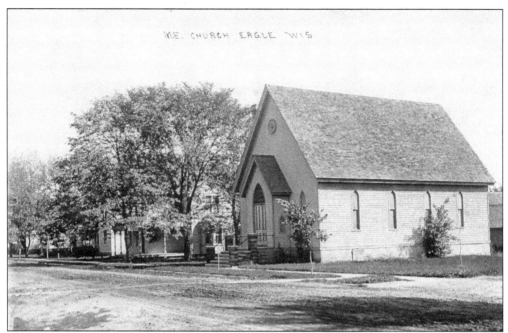

SECOND METHODIST CHURCH. The current location is A on the village map on page 32. The earliest pioneers held services in their houses. In 1860, John Hage purchased the original Eagle Centre schoolhouse (D on page 32) and preached there for 11 years. In 1871, the new church was built and has been there ever since. A new addition was built on the church in the mid-1950s on land donated by Roy Wambold.

ST. THERESA'S CATHOLIC CHURCH, C. 1910. In 1852, a small frame church was erected, and services were provided in German and English. In 1870, the first parsonage was erected, and the congregation received a resident pastor. The current church's cornerstone was laid in 1895, and the dedication took place in 1896. (EHS.)

SILOAM CHURCH. Although currently in Palmyra, Jefferson County, the original wooden church was built in 1851 on the opposite corner of the intersection within Section 6 of the northwest corner of Eagle and supported Melendy's Prairie. The church was originally a Canadian Bible Christian Society, which was similar to the Church of England. It withdrew from the Canadian Conference and united with the Methodist Episcopal Church in 1884. The new church was completed in 1870. (Author's collection.)

BAPTIST CHURCH. The Baptist church was organized in 1870. It utilized the building that was the first school in Eagle Centre and then the original Methodist church location (D). The congregation started with seven people and never exceeded 35. No images of it could be found, but it was probably basic and looked like this church from a nearby town. (Author's collection.)

PALESTINE SCHOOL DISTRICT 1, 1928. In 1836, Ahira Hinkley leased land at a dollar a year to build a school near Palestine. Around 1846, a log school was built, which was replaced in 1854 with a wood-frame school. In 1928, the frame school was replaced by a brick building. Palestine School was the last multigrade, one-room schoolhouse in Wisconsin when it was discontinued in 1970. It continued as a Kindergarten until 1986, when it closed as the last single-room school in Wisconsin. (EHS.)

MELENDY'S PRAIRIE STONE SCHOOL, DISTRICT 2. In 1845, a wooden, one-room schoolhouse was built on Melendy's Prairie. In 1855, it was replaced with a school of colored stones by John B. Chapin, a stonemason from Vermont. Pictured here is an unknown class in front of that school. In 1952, the district dissolved, and the school became part of a private residence that was lived in by Chapin's great-grandson Thomas Burton. (Ryan Hajewski.)

WARD SCHOOL, DISTRICT 3. Ward School was opened in 1849 and has been in the same place ever since. In 1957, it was consolidated with the village school because of being outdated, such as still having outdoor toilets. The building is typical of the small country schoolhouses built by the first Yankee farmers and is the oldest remaining schoolhouse in Waukesha County. It is located in the living history museum Old World Wisconsin. (Author's collection.)

EAGLEVILLE SCHOOL, DISTRICT 4. The school district was formed in 1849, but the first school was not built for over 10 years because the Uphills and Downhills bickered over which side of the hill the school should be built on. In 1860, a 24-by-30-foot school was erected on the Uphill side on the northwest corner of Sprague Road and CTH LO on land donated by Matthias Bovee. In the autumn of 1869, it was moved to Downhill by Romeo Sprague for $50.

JERICHO SCHOOL DISTRICT 6, 1969. The school district began in 1849 with Gertrude Goodrich as the first teacher. Jericho was the second to last one-room school still open in Wisconsin when it closed in 1969. There were 22 students in the last class. During the late 1800s, a nondenominational Sunday school was also taught at the school. (The Mukwonago Historical Society.)

SECOND VILLAGE SCHOOL DISTRICT 9, C. 1900. District 9 encompasses Eagle Centre and was organized in 1846. The first school (D) was a 24-by-30-foot, 12-foot-tall balloon frame, single-room schoolhouse that was completed during the winter of 1850–1851. Shown here is the second school that was built in 1858 on the south side of Eagle. It was destroyed by fire when lightning struck it in 1905. (Roxanne Raduechel-Butler.)

WALKING TO SCHOOL, C. 1930. From left to right, neighbors Betty Cruver, June Sprague, and Norma Smart are shown walking to Eagleville School. These girls walked the 1.3 miles to school every day while growing up. They may have had shortcuts through the farm fields to get the trip down to one mile.

WALKING TO SCHOOL, C. 1935. From left to right, Norma Smart, Betty Cruver, and June Sprague walk to Eagleville school when they are a bit older. Although these pictures show nice weather, there were many cold, snowy, rainy, or windy days when they still had to walk to school.

TOWN OF EAGLE.

Second Infantry—Co. K—Nicholas Hanes, Chas. Brown. Company unknown—Elberton Bigelow.
Fourth Infantry—Co. A—Peter Hunter, James Cardle.
Fifth Infantry—Co. F— ——Gilchrist. Co. K—Wallace Root.
Thirteenth Infantry—Co. I—John Miller, Henry Carle, John Hubbard, Joshua Scott. Co. K—Napoleon B. Draper, Wm. Kanute.
Sixteenth Infantry—J. D. Reed. Co. I—P. V. Bovee.
Seventeenth Infantry—Co. B—Conrad Van Readen, Bernhart Meyer, John Fink. John Briedenback, Anton Schulte, Martin Schulte, Jacob Van Readen, Martin Devine, Hiram Daniels, Bernhart Briedenback, John Stinoff.
Twenty-fourth Infantry—Co. A—Sidney Kline, George Logan, Franklin W. Rice, Mathias J. Bovee, Jr., Stephen W. Powell, John I. Bovee, William B. Sherman, Lewis M. Sherman, Leonard D. Hinkley, Mathias L. Snyder and Thomas Lewis.
Twenty-eighth Infantry—Company unknown—Wilson Kipp, John Kalp, William Harrison, Albert Williams, John Nelson, Michael O'Neil, William Lean, Jeremiah Carr, John McIntyre, Edward P. Hinkley, William Duncan, John Cummins, C. J. Melenda.
First Cavalry—Co. A—Thomas Audis. Co. K—Thomas S. Draper, Wm. Logan, Charles Kilts, Frank Snover, H. F. Potter. Company unknown—Frank Bigelow, James Grant, James Robison, Jeremiah Bessey, Julius Mastic.
Third Cavalry—Co. D—Henry James, Henry Brewin, Thomas Pryor, William Keener, Timothy Sullivan, L. W. Robison, Hiram Lampman, Caleb Lobdell, William Lobdell, Martin Lee.
Seventh Battery—Charles Willard, Frank Fox, George Alvord, Edgar Wainright, John Burke, Arthur Wainright, Walter Downing, Samuel Kinder.
First Heavy Artillery—Andrew J. Reeves, Myron Scott, Edward O'Brien, Norman Markley, Silas Reeves, John Western, David Kinder, Thomas Lacey.
Second Heavy Artillery—Seymour Lewis.
Langworthy Artillery—Francis Draper, Jr., William Bigelow, Benson Sternes.
Regiment unknown—Clesant Hendrickson, E. P.

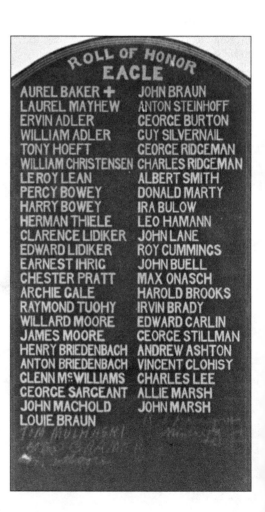

EAGLE'S CIVIL WAR VETERANS. Shown are some of Eagle's residents who served during the Civil War. The 24th Infantry Regiment was commanded by Lt. Col. Arthur MacArthur Jr., who later became a general. Arthur received the Medal of Honor for rallying Union troops at the Battle of Missionary Ridge by charging up a ridge, yelling, "On, Wisconsin!" This would later be turned into Wisconsin's state song. Arthur was the father of the famous World War II leader Gen. Douglas MacArthur. (University of Wisconsin–Madison.)

EAGLE'S WORLD WAR I VETERANS, 1918. Eagle's World War I memorial has been lost to time, but a similar granite memorial is at the Eagle Historical Society. Many of the families still have descendants in the area although their names have changed through marriages. The penciled-in names are people who enlisted shortly after the official ending of the war.

WORLD WAR II MEMORIAL, 1943. This is Eagle's World War II memorial. The preserved memorial with additional names is at the Eagle Historical Society. Many of the family names were early pioneer families and still have descendants in the area.

EAGLES AMERICAN LEGION POST 535. The Sargent-Splecter-Schmidt American Legion was organized in 1948. George Sargent lost his life from the flu contracted at Fort Leavenworth, Kansas, in 1918. Francis Splecter died in action in the Battle of the Bulge in 1944. Ens. Thomas Schmidt drowned at sea in a flying operation in 1932. The drill team was organized in 1951. Trained by Kenneth Mealy, it won numerous awards competing in the surrounding area.

NORTH PRAIRIE FIRE DEPARTMENT, C. 1935. An early 1920s Ford Model T firetruck is pictured with the North Prairie Fire Department, which was established in 1934. North Prairie is a village on the northeast edge of the town of Eagle. Like Eagle Centre, it also prospered by getting a train station in 1851.

FIREMAN AT PALESTINE SCHOOL, 1929. Volunteer firefighters pose for a photograph in front of the Palestine school. From left to right are (first row) George Pitcher, Arthur Stocks, Henry Markham, Waldo Shearer, Joe Bock, Warren Cruver, Frank Breidenbach, Carl "Butch" Belling, Joe Mealy, Dean Jones, Earl Crawley, Millard Markham, and Jerome Mealy Sr.; (second row) Dick Gibson, Ray Alpress, Everett Amman, Harvey Wambold, Ken Mealy, Bob Breidenbach, unidentified, and Frank Mich.

DR. SPRAGUE'S WISCONSIN BALM, 1850. Dr. Sprague was a homeopathic doctor who settled on the Southeast corner of Eagle Centre in Section 23. This was an advertisement for one of his medicines. His descendants still live on the Eagle Prairie, but the knowledge of this special plant was not passed down. The first apprentice-trained doctor was C.B. Bannister, who opened a practice in Eagle in 1866 that lasted until the late 1880s. (Author's collection.)

EXTRACT OF WISCONSIN BALM, For colds, cough, consumption, pain in the sides or chest, croup or rattles, &c.

THE Wisconsin Balm was first discovered by Dr. Sprague, of Eagle Prairie, in 1844, since that itme thousands have been saved from an untimely grave by the use of the Extract of that invaluable herb. The demand for this extract has been such that no effort has been spared to discover this plant in other parts of the state, but as yet it has been found only on Eagle Prairie. The Extract may be used with perfect safety, and is one of the best medicines for children, as well as adults, ever yet discovered, and many parents do affirm that this Extract is the only medicine they have used in their families for several years.

☞ Sold by most of the Druggists in the county

EAGLE HOSPITAL. Dr. James Fitzgerald practiced in Eagle from 1895 to 1932. Originally, his practice was downtown (F) but was moved to the Eagle Hospital in 1914 (B). Dr. Frederick Schmidt joined the practice in 1912. The hospital closed due to a shortage of nurses and the ability of patients to drive to Waukesha. The home is now a private residence (EHS.)

ROAD MAINTENANCE, C. 1920. Early roads were no more than packed dirt, which the farmers would be paid by the town to maintain. This was a symbiotic relationship, since the farmers needed to get their goods to market and the town did not have road workers. In this photograph, it is believed that the farmers are plowing the dirt to raise the road and create a ditch for drainage.

ROAD LEVELING, C. 1935. Paul Kramer Sr. (1903–1939) is on a 1920s Wehr power grader leveling a road in Eagle. Leveling gravel was a continual responsibility until the roads were asphalted starting in 1930 and finalized in 1958. The Milwaukee-based Wehr Steel Corporation mated its grader with a Fordson tractor.

ROAD SNOW PLOWING. The first county snowplowing began in the 1920s. Prior to that, horses pulled sleighs over the snow for travel. As automobiles became more prevalent, their poor ability to travel through snow required the roads to be plowed. Paul Kramer Sr. is in the center, flanked by two unidentified men.

SPRAGUE ROAD FLOODING, C. 1935. This view looks north on Sprague Road about halfway between NN and LO. The road here would flood from time to time until it was raised in the 1950s using dirt from the hill in front of the Sprague Farm. "Cruver," shown on the mailbox, was I.P. Walker's farm in Section 23; the farm in the background was not shown on the 1859 town map. Notice how few trees were on the prairie at that time.

ELECTION DAY. Poll workers are shown ready to ensure the integrity of the election process. Back then, everyone knew everyone, and a visual confirmation was probably sufficient. It is unknown if this was the town or village or even which election this was for.

EAGLE TOWN BOARD, C. 1935. Pictured here is the Eagle town board; from left to right are supervisors Henry Loibl and James Bovee, clerk Charles Cruver, treasurer Sidney Sprague, assessor John Marty, and supervisors Giles Lean and Anton Steinhoff.

EAGLE TELEPHONE COMPANY, C. 1902. This parade float advertises telephone service. The Eagle Telephone Company was founded in 1902 by Edmund Lins Jr. (1865–1921) with a capital stock of $3,000. It employed five girls for clerical and telephonic service, operated seven exchanges, and served 1,000 subscribers. The company was purchased by the Northwest Company shortly after Lins's death. A switchboard from the telephone company can be found at the Eagle Museum.

RURAL FREE DELIVERY, C. 1910. William Logan (1839–1925) is shown in front of his mail carriage and horse. Rural Free Delivery was enacted in 1896, which allowed mail and catalogs to be delivered to people's houses in rural areas. Before that, people needed to pick up their mail at the post office. Route 35 served 385 people in 77 houses across 24 miles on the north side of Eagle. (EHS.)

VILLAGE OF EAGLE LIBRARY. In 1905, Martin Bovee dedicated a room in his store for Eagle's first library. In the 1970s, Alice Baker organized a small library in a classroom of the Methodist church. In 1984, Carl Zipprich donated the Partridge house, shown here, as a library. This building is now home to the Eagle Historical Society, and the library moved to its current location in 1994. (Tom Shropshire.)

EAGLE ADVANCEMENT ASSOCIATION. The association began in 1903 and supported the village in many ways, such as building sidewalks, sponsoring Christmas trees, and purchasing benches and firefighting equipment. It was incorporated in the 1950s, with few details about what happened to it after that. It was restarted in 2019 to replace the playground equipment in the Village Park.

Eight

PEOPLE

This book could not have been written without the people of Eagle, which is why they are the grand finale of the book. Many of the people were either pioneers or descendants of pioneers who risked everything to move west. Some came through the Great Lakes, some followed Indian trails, and others created new trails. They endured the hardships of breaking new soil and growing crops while living in a wagon and building a house to survive their first winter. They did all this with only what they took with them and had few neighbors or social support to help them in emergencies. They were not just farmers but had to do every job to survive and thus are deserving of the title of pioneer.

These pioneers blazed the trails and created the social structure for settlers to have an "easier" life. The farmers adapted to the unfamiliar soil types and climate, experimented with crops, animals, and machinery, and persevered. With the growth of the town, specialized professions moved in, such as millers, bankers, butchers, shop owners, blacksmiths, carpenters, cheesemakers, and many others.

Although the population has steadily climbed, it does not show how many people have truly lived in Eagle. Reviewing census records, up to 70 percent of the town would turn over each decade, making the town and village's 2010 population of 5,549 pale in comparison to the tens of thousands of people who have lived in Eagle since its founding.

Every one of those people had a story, and many of them could have been put into this book. Unfortunately, most of those stories have been lost to time. Presented here is a sampling of Eagle's families and their stories.

It is amazing that even with such high turnover and after 180-plus years and eight-plus generations, there are still descendants of a few of the pioneer families. Those found so far include Betts, Bigelow, Bovee, Brady, Burden, Clemons, Cole, Ely, Ewer, Gose, Hinkley, McCabe, Parsons, Pittman, Sprague, and Wambold.

BAKER FAMILY. Francis Baker (1845–1926) immigrated with his family from Cornwall, England, to Troy, Wisconsin, in 1849. He moved to Eagle sometime before 1880, farming 158 acres off Betts Road in Section 33. Seen here is his daughter Alice (1882–1974), who became a teacher in 1910. She taught in Montana, China, Eagleville, and a few other places, ending her career in 1945. She contributed numerous articles to local newspapers, which have been valuable assets to this book. She heavily advocated for a local library during her lifetime. The library was posthumously named in her honor. Francis's son John Earle Baker (1880–1957) was appointed by President Truman as chief of the Joint Rural Reconstruction Commission of China and spent 34 years there.

BETTS FAMILY, 1939. Jonathan Betts (1813–1891) came from England in 1830 and moved to Eagle in 1838. He operated a six-yoke oxen sod breaking plow and plowed thousands of acres of virgin prairie sod. He had a 160-acre farm in Section 33 off Betts Road, which was named for his family. Pictured here are Vivian (left, 1922–1999) and Fremont Betts (1922–1995), great-grandchildren of the pioneers Jonathan Betts and John Burden. They are providing a milking cleanliness demonstration at the Wisconsin State Fair. They won first prize and a trip to California to present the demonstration. Their descendants still live in the area.

MATTHIAS BOVEE. Shown is a pendant with the image of Congressman Matthias Bovee (1793–1872). He was born in New Amsterdam, New York, and his father died when he was 14. He served in the New York militia during the 1820s. He was a schoolteacher and merchant who became involved with railroads, banks, and local government. He was a Jacksonian congressman from 1835 to 1837. In 1843, he moved to Eagle with his mother, wife, and nine children, where he became a farmer. His mother, Jane, was the first settler to die in Eagle. Five of his children—Benedict, Marvin H., Halsey, William, and Sarah (who married Thomas Pittman)—continued farming in Eagle, owning over 1,500 acres. Marvin became a state senator and was instrumental in abolishing the state's death penalty. Numerous descendants still live in the area, and Matthias is the author's fourth great-grandfather.

BOVEE FAMILY, C. 1918. Pictured here are the fourth and fifth generations of Bovees in Eagle. From left to right are (first row) Marvin W. (1859–1947) and Margaret née Robinson (1858–1943); (second row) Katherine (1897–2000), Benedict Arthur (1889–1985), Myrtle née Manwaring (Benedict's wife, 1891–1983), James (1895–1992), and Frances (1900–1919). Jim's grandson lives on the land originally settled by Jim's great grandfather Matthias, making it a sesquicentennial farm (150-plus years in the same family).

THREE GENERATIONS OF COLLINS-MARTY FAMILY, C. 1910. From left to right are Fern Marty (1895–1990); her mother, Lillian Marty née Collins (1871–1942); and grandmother Jane Collins née Smith (1848–1930). Fern married James Bovee. Lilian Married John Marty (1868–1943), a Swiss who settled in Eagle around 1905 and had a large farm on the northwest corner of E and NN in Jericho. Jane and her husband, John, immigrated to the United States in 1870 from England and lived in Green County.

Michael Brady. Michael Brady (1817–1881) immigrated to New York State from Ireland in 1842, married Catherine McCabe in 1850, and moved to Eagle in 1855. He purchased 160 acres with a 12-by-12-foot cabin on it in Sections 9 and 10. He also operated a quarry known as Bradys Rocks, which is now part of the Southern Kettle Moraine. His granddaughter Mary Brady married Jesse Sprague, and their descendants still live in Eagle. Michael is the author's third great-grandfather.

The Ely Family, c. 1910. Edwin Ely (1859–1943) and daughters, from left to right, Bessie (1898–1999), Ruth (1901–1923), and Isabelle (1896–1956) pose for a photograph. Their mother, Clara Brimmer, passed away in 1903. They had a 200-acre farm in Section 25 on the east side of Sprague Road. Edwin was born in Eagle to New York native John Ely and Eagle native Juliett Sprague, who was a daughter of Frederick. No descendants have been found in Eagle.

THE BURDEN FAMILY. John Burden (1816–1883), wife Mary, and their seven children came to America from Cornwall, England, in 1857. They farmed in Palmyra and then Waukesha. In 1868, they exchanged farms with Hy Kipp in Section 24 on the southwest corner of Jericho. In the late 1870s, Burden purchased another 128 acres from William Bingham Sprague (1838–1909), Frederic Sprague's son, in Section 26. This brought his farms up to 360 acres. His son Edward married Ada Sprague (1863–1937), the daughter of William. Records show Edward using both the Burton and Burden family names and his descendants using the Burton name, even though they are not related to the other Burton family in Eagle. It is unknown why the name was changed. Their son Edward "Ned" Burton (1889–1944), pictured here, was a farmer, postmaster, and insurance agent as well as chairman of the Republican State Committee. Ned's obituary is filled with prominent politicians, including the former Wisconsin governor Julius P. Heil. Heil founded the Heil Company of Milwaukee in 1901, which is still in business today, producing refuse trucks.

THE GOSA FAMILY. Frederick Gosa Sr. (1820–1889) was born in Westphalia, Prussia, where he spent three years in the army. He became a tailor and immigrated to Milwaukee in 1848. In 1853, he settled on 80 acres on Sections 17 and 21 in Eagle, where he built a house and increased his land holdings to 220 acres. He married Elizabeth Whiffen from his home country and had nine children. His son Frederick Gosa Jr. (1854–1888) and Theresa Kalb (1865–1941) are shown here. Descendants still live in the Waukesha area. While researching this book, Frederick Jr.'s great-great-grandson found out he briefly lived in the same house the family settled in without knowing it.

THE PARSONS FAMILY. In 1836, Jonathan Parsons and his children—Samos, Jon Jr., Louisa, and Jerry—migrated to Eagle from New Hampshire. Jerry married Emily Bovee, daughter of Matthias Bovee, and established a hotel in Jericho that he operated until leaving for the California gold rush in 1849. Jon Jr., whose portrait is seen here, was a member of the territorial legislature and willed $500 of his land to the Methodist Church. His marriage to Jane Cross in 1841 was the first in the town. His descendants still live in the area. (Eagle Methodist Church.)

THE HINKLEY FAMILY. After Ahira Hinkley settled in Eagle, he returned to New Hampshire to get consent for his sweetheart to move to Wisconsin. They were a prominent family that felt that living in the Wisconsin frontier with its Indians and hardships "was little better than signing a death warrant." Ahira's cousin Oramel (1812–1855) and his wife, Phoebe née Earl (1810–1879), settled in Section 10 and had 160 acres. Their descendants still live in the area. (EHS.)

WILLIAM KNIGHT, 1882–1943. William Knight was a renowned breeder of Jersey cows and showed them across the Midwest, where he won numerous awards at state fairs. Jersey cows originated on the British island Jersey and are known for their milk with high butterfat content, which is a benefit in cheese and butter making.

ENOLA KNIGHT NÉE BURDEN, 1878–1968. Enola was the grandchild of the pioneer John Burden. She married William Knight in 1905, who moved to Eagle to work for her father, William Henry Burden. They owned the former Parsons farm in Section 25 and called it the Oak Grove Dairy Farm. The farm has a beautiful cream-colored brick farmhouse and barn on Highway E between Jericho and Eagleville.

THE LINS FAMILY. John August "J.A." Lins (1840–1905) was born in Prussia and came to America in 1857. He was shot during the Civil War. After the war, he was a butcher and mercantilist and owned an elevator and Paradise Springs. He also served as a state senator. Pictured here is his brother Edmund Lins (1827–1923), who operated the saloon, bowling alley, beer bottling plant, and meat market. The third brother, Charles (1824–1873), died young, but his son Charles Jr. (1857–1903) operated the hardware, drugstore, and telephone exchange. (EHS.)

EDMUND LINS

REPORT OF SENIOR VICE COMMANDER

M. L. SNYDER
Senior Vice Commander

MATTHIAS SNYDER, 1842–1923. Born in Prussia, Matthias Snyder immigrated to America with his family in 1844. During his three years in the Civil War, he fought in 18 battles. He served as Eagle's town clerk, clerk of the circuit court, sheriff of Waukesha County, chairman of the county board, commander of the Waukesha and State Grand Army of the Republic, veterans' societies, and as mayor of Waukesha from 1904 to 1908. He married Amelia Gosa, daughter of Frederick Gosa, and they had nine children. (EHS.)

Dr. Frederick Augustus Sprague, 1794–1865. Frederick, wife Bridget, and their nine children came from Malden, Massachusetts, via Richfield, Ohio. He came from a prominent family who founded Malden and had an ancestor who served in the Revolutionary War. He served during the War of 1812 as a colonel in the Ohio Militia. In 1842, the family settled on 200 acres just east of what would later become the village of Eagle. The doctor and four of his sons ultimately owned over 740 acres in Eagle He served as a state senator from 1849 to 1850. Numerous descendants still live in the area, and Dr. Sprague is the author's fourth great-grandfather.

Joseph Sprague, 1825–1896. Joseph was the third oldest of Dr. Sprague's 11 children. He originally farmed around Paradise Springs. He married Ann Bovee (1829–1875), the daughter of Mathias Bovee, and they had three children. In 1855, he bought 160 acres from his brother-in-law William Bovee in Section 26 for $4,000. Five generations later, this farm is still in the family as a sesquicentennial farm.

The Sprague Family. Shown are the third and fourth generation of Spragues in Eagle. From left to right are (first row) Frances and Theodore (1848–1924); (second row) Jesse, Alice, Sidney, Delia, and Oren. Theodore worked for his father Joseph on the farm until he took over. His oldest son, Jesse, married Mary Brady, granddaughter of pioneer Michael Brady, and took over the Sprague farm. Sidney was the town treasurer and a photographer.

THE STEAD FAMILY. Henry Stead (1832–1890) was born in England and came to America around 1848 with his parents. He was a farmer until he had "paralytic shock," from which he never fully recovered. To make ends meet, he ran a small grocery store in Eagle. He married Mary Smart (1841–1911) and had four children: Annie (1863–1943), Arthur (1865–1935), Sylvia (1867–1958), and Jay (1883–1969). Mary operated the confectionary that was razed in 1905. Sylvia married James Sherman, who ran Eagle's grocery store. Arthur farmed until he was appointed as a mail messenger. He also served as town and village treasurer. Jay was a rural mail carrier and mortician. His wife, Charlotte Bigelow, was the first matron of the Masonic lodge. His daughter Mary Lou married Red Hinkley, connecting various pioneer families.

THE STUTE FAMILY. Frank Stute (c. 1797–1889) immigrated from Prussia with his wife, Anna, and nine children in 1852. He built a log cabin on 180 acres in Section 30. His children Anton (1843–1923) and Theresa (1846–1946) married Von Rueden siblings, another large Eagle family. In 1880, their log cabin was replaced with a frame house. Anton's son Joseph and family, pictured here, farmed their land until 1943. In 1982, the state purchased the farm and razed the buildings in 1996. The land has been returned to nature as part of the Southern Kettle Moraine Forest. The Stute Springs and Homestead Trail are portions of the homestead. From left to right are (first row) Joseph and Agatha née Weiler; (second row) Anton, Clara, Helen Gertrude, Catherine, Frances, and Clement ("Buddy"). Descendants still live in the Eagle area. (Nora Fuller.).

THE VON RUEDEN FAMILY REUNION. In 1852, Jacob Von Rueden (1793–1860), wife Theresa (1801–1853), and their four sons and two daughters came to Eagle from Germany. Sons Frederick (1833–1917), Joseph (1835–1916), and Johann Bernard (1837–1879) stayed in the western portion of Eagle, owning 332 acres in Sections 19, 30, and 31 in 1873. Their farms were sold to the state in 1963 and are now part of the Southern Kettle Moraine. The original homestead lived in by Jacob, Frederick, and Joseph was saved and is listed in the State Register of Historic Places and was known as the Eagle Home Hostel. Frederick was a town supervisor for two years. As can be seen in this photograph of a family reunion, they had a very large family. The descendants married numerous familiar family names, too many to outline here, but descendants are still in the area.

THE WAMBOLD FAMILY. Harvey Wambold (1926–1908) settled in Eagleville in 1871, purchasing a five-year lease on the mill and waterpower. He owned 160 acres on the east side of Eagle Springs Lake in Section 36; all but 42 acres were underwater. In 1899, the mill was sold to Harvey's son Leander (1860–1933), who also raised pigs around Eagle Springs. In 1915, A.C. Clark sued Leander for the foul-smelling animals, which was ultimately settled in favor of Leander in 1917 by the Wisconsin Supreme Court. There is currently a Wambold Road on the east side of Eagle Springs Lake, which travels over the Wambold Dam. This picture is of Ramona Wambold (1934–2014), the granddaughter of Leander. Descendants still reside in the Eagle area.

Bibliography

Atlas of Waukesha County. Madison, WI: Harrison & Warner, 1873.
Baker, Alice. *History of Eagle, WI.* Eagle, WI: Eagle Historical Society, 2008, 2009.
Waukesha Freeman Centennial Edition. March 29, 1959.
dnr.wi.gov
Clayton, Lee. *Pleistocene Geology of Waukesha County, Wisconsin.* University of Wisconsin-Extension, Wisconsin Geological and Natural History Survey, 2001.
"Eagle Walking Tour." Eagle, WI: Eagle Historical Society, 2018.
Fuller, Nora Stute. *Growing up on a Family Farm in the 1940's and 50's.* Eagle, WI: 2010.
Haight, Theron W., ed. *Memoirs of Waukesha County.* Madison, WI: Western Historical Association, 1907.
History of Waukesha County. Chicago, IL: Western Historical Company, 1880.
Luczaj, John A. *Geology of the Niagara Escarpment in Wisconsin: Geoscience Wisconsin,* v.22 part 1, pp. 1–34. University of Wisconsin Green Bay, 2013.
Map of the County of Waukesha Wisconsin. New York, NY: M.H Tyler, 1859.
"Paradise Springs Self-Guiding Nature Trail." Madison, WI: Wisconsin Department of Natural Resources, 2015.
Portrait and Biographical Record of Waukesha County, Wisconsin. Chicago, IL: Excelsior Publishing Company, 1894.
Pierce, Clara Howell. *Historical Gleanings of Melendy's Prairie from 1836–1970.* Palmyra, WI: Palmyra Historical Society, 1970.
"Thrifty Eagle." *Waukesha Freeman.* Waukesha, WI: February 23, 1893.
www.loc.gov
"Stute Springs and Homestead." Madison, WI: Wisconsin Department of Natural Resources.

INDEX

Baker, Alice, 45, 108, 110
Betts, Jonathan, 14, 109, 111
Bigelow, Daniel, 15, 20, 109
Bovee, Frances, 48, 57, 78, 113
Bovee, James, 48, 78, 79, 85, 92, 106, 113
Bovee, Katherine, 48, 57, 78, 113
Bovee, Marvin, 26, 112, 113
Bovee, Matthias, 40, 97, 112, 113, 117, 121
Brady, Michael, 13, 109, 114, 121
Burden, John, 18, 109, 111, 115
Civil War, 10, 61, 100, 119
Clark, A.C., 22, 81, 125
Clark's Park, 22, 81, 82, 91
Clemons, Harvey, 33, 34, 109
Cruver, Betty, 99
Cruver, Charles, 64, 106
Eagle Springs Golf Resort, 14, 24, 25, 50, 83
Eagle Springs Lake, 20–25, 31, 50, 52, 53, 77, 78, 79, 83, 85, 91, 125
Eagleville, 2, 8, 10, 15, 20, 21, 48, 66, 79, 81, 82, 86, 87, 97, 99, 110, 118, 125
Ely, Edwin, 62, 109, 114
Ely, Isabelle, 25, 48, 50, 114
Gosa, Frederick, 116, 119
Harley Davidson, 45, 49
Hinkley, Ahira, 15, 30, 31, 96, 109, 117
Ice Age Trail, 13, 77, 89
Jericho, 2, 8, 9, 10, 15, 18, 19, 69, 75, 87, 98, 113, 115, 117, 118
Lins, Charles, 43, 119
Lins, Edmund, 43, 107, 119
Lins, J.A., 23, 26, 36, 43, 119
Marty, Don, 60, 79, 80, 81, 100, 101
Marty, John, 106, 113
Melendy, Daniel, 15, 29
Melendy's Prairie, 2, 8, 15, 29, 95, 96
Michaelis, Donald, 19, 101
Michaelis, William, 19, 49
Mukwonago, 8, 10, 15, 21, 42, 66, 75, 83, 98
Native Americans, 8, 11, 14
North Prairie, 80, 102
Old World Wisconsin, 20, 97
Ottawa, 29, 80
Pabst, August, 28
Palestine, 2, 8, 10, 15, 30, 96, 102
Palmyra, 29, 95, 115
Paradise Springs, 7, 14, 26–29, 77, 87, 119, 121
Petit, Louis, 27, 28
Pittman, Thomas, 31, 109, 112
Pratt, Chester, 48, 85, 100
Rockteacher, Lizzie, 51
Sherman, Vinton, 47
Smart, Harry, 42
Snyder, Matthias, 100, 119
Sprague, Alice, 46, 56, 57, 67, 121
Sprague, Delia, 21, 25, 46, 48, 50, 57, 67, 72, 78, 88, 121
Sprague, Frances, 46, 56, 57, 121
Sprague, Frederick, 8, 103, 114, 115, 120
Sprague, Jesse, 46, 53, 54, 63–67, 70, 74, 76, 78–81, 85, 90, 92, 114, 121
Sprague, Joseph, 26, 78, 121
Sprague, June, 73, 86, 99
Sprague, Sidney, 4, 6, 48, 55, 60, 89, 121
Stead, Jay, 43, 122
Steinhoff, Anton, 81, 100, 104, 106
Tuohy, Agnes, 24, 25, 48, 50, 83
Tuohy, Mary, 25, 50, 83
Von Rueden, Jacob, 124
Wambold, Harvey, 20, 49, 79, 101, 109, 100, 125

DISCOVER THOUSANDS OF LOCAL HISTORY BOOKS FEATURING MILLIONS OF VINTAGE IMAGES

Arcadia Publishing, the leading local history publisher in the United States, is committed to making history accessible and meaningful through publishing books that celebrate and preserve the heritage of America's people and places.

Find more books like this at
www.arcadiapublishing.com

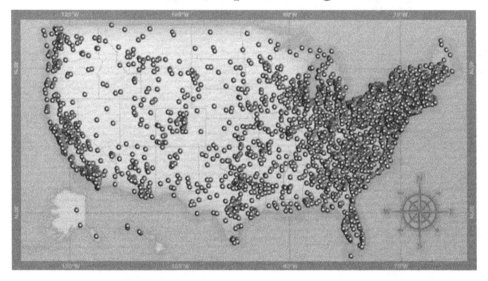

Search for your hometown history, your old stomping grounds, and even your favorite sports team.

Consistent with our mission to preserve history on a local level, this book was printed in South Carolina on American-made paper and manufactured entirely in the United States. Products carrying the accredited Forest Stewardship Council (FSC) label are printed on 100 percent FSC-certified paper.

CPSIA information can be obtained
at www.ICGtesting.com
Printed in the USA
BVHW010016090622
639245BV00001B/17